I Am Somebody

Sixth Edition

By
Anna Leider
and the staff of Educational Access

Cover Design by Supon Design
Book Design by Edington-Rand

Address correspondence to:
Octameron Associates
PO Box 2748
Alexandria, VA 22301
703/836-5480

Address bookstore inquiries regarding purchases and returns to:
Dearborn Trade
520 N. Dearborn Street
Chicago, IL 60610
Outside Illinois, 800/245-BOOK
In Illinois, 312/654-8596 x270

ISBN 0-945981-94-5
PRINTED IN THE UNITED STATES OF AMERICA

CONTENTS

Foreword to Parents   4

Chapter 1   Martin Luther King, Jr., Jesse Jackson, Charlotte Wilhite and You   8

Chapter 2   Meet Some Young People Who Made It — You Can, Too!   11

Chapter 3   Good Reasons for Going to College   14

Chapter 4   Some Things You Believe About College Just Aren't So   19

Chapter 5   What You Need to Know About College Selection & Admission   32

Chapter 6   What You Need to Know About Financial Aid   53

Chapter 7   A Senior Year Time Table   62

Chapter 8   Application Money, Resources, Writing Letters, Helpful People . . .   65

Chapter 9   Model Programs that Work: A Chapter for Teachers and Counselors   69

Chapter 10   A Last Thought   73

Worksheets   74

Glossary   81

ACKNOWLEDGMENTS

Research for the original edition of this publication was funded by the US Department of Education's Fund for the Improvement for Post-secondary Education under Grant G008302531.

The contents of the publication, however, do not necessarily reflect the views or policies of the US Department of Education, nor does mention of institutions, publications, organizations, and programs therein imply endorsement by the US Government.

The grantee, Educational Access, and its professional staff are solely responsible for the contents of the publication.

PROJECT STAFF

Anna Leider, President, Educational Access   *Co-Project Director*
Robert Leider, Educational Access   *Co-Project Director*
Mrs. Dorothea Slocum, Director and Founder,
     Operation College-Bound, Washington DC   *Senior Consultant*
Edward B. Wall, Partner, Gibbs and Wall,
     Educational Counselors   *Senior Consultant*

The staff of Educational Access would like to thank the following college admission and financial aid officers for providing us with thumbnail sketches of students who have succeeded and sample financial aid packages for students from disadvantaged backgrounds:

Robert L. Baily, Michael C. Behnke, William R. Bennett, George C. Brooks, Kathleen Bush, Richard Cashwell, Catherine E. Clack, Evelyn B. Finck, David M. Flynn, Vernon L. Francis, John V. Griffith, Rodney A. Hart, Thomas B. Martin, James J. Scannell, Richard C. Skelton, Sylvia V. Terry, Richard J. Toomey, Elizabeth G. Vermey, Phyllis Washington-Stone, Jimmy Williams,

We would also like to thank the following high school counselors for their invaluable assistance:

Linden Beckford, Queen Boyd, Carolyn Briscoe, P. Drummond, Starlee Hamme, Phyllis Hart, Gwendolyn Hoover, Dr. Phillip Jeunette, Eleanor Jones, Annette Levey, Barry Liebman, C. McClintock, Carolyn Milam, Lorraine Monroe, Don Mrsocak, Clarence Nemhardt, Florence Ridley, Eva Rousseau, Cheryl Rutherford, Nancy Scott, Allen Smith, Tony Solorzano, Jesus Sosa, B. Weavers, Jack Wright.

Foreword to Parents

Young people are the life blood of our society. With them comes the hope for better communities and a brighter future for all. The key to unlocking this brighter future is education—a college education.

Getting a job right out of high school may seem appealing to your child, or it may seem necessary in order for your family to make ends meet. But in the long run it is not the best move for your child, or your family.

As technology continues to advance, the job market for unskilled labor continues to shrink. For someone without extra training or education, only dead end and low paying jobs will be available, if any at all. A college education changes that. It qualifies your child for a job with a future—one that pays well and is secure; one that benefits your community. America needs your children to become its teachers, its doctors and its lawyers.

A college education provides the skills and confidence your child will need to survive in this world; skills and confidence which are just as important for your daughter as they are for your son. Your daughter still has an important role as wife and mother, the essential link of the "familia," but today her role is complicated as she must also work to help pay her family's bills. A college education will enable her to contribute to her family as well as her community.

Let your child go away to school, even if it's far away from home. Your child will be safe, not alone and unprotected. College housing is carefully arranged and supervised, meal plans are well established, and support services of all types abound—especially for African-American, Chicano and Latino ethnic groups. Going away to school will help your son or daughter mature and learn to deal effectively with all kinds of people. Going away to school will also strengthen family and community ties. No college wants its students to abandon their families or their cultural, ethnic and racial heritage. In fact, colleges encourage diversity in their student body as a means to promote better understanding amongst all people.

Don't let your financial situation prevent you from seeking a college education for your child. Money is available from the state and federal government and from any college your child wishes to attend. To receive this money, however, you must fill out an application form. These applications are available at your child's high school. The questions are sometimes complicated, but your child's guidance counselor will be able to help you. Remember, this form must be filled out, and filled out accurately, for you to receive financial assistance. College is expensive and almost no one is able to complete four years without this kind of assistance. The money is there for the benefit of your children. This is America's way of investing in its citizens and thereby investing in its future. *There is nothing shameful about accepting it.*

This booklet will explain the college admission and financial aid process in more detail. It will remove other concerns you may have. And it will tell you where to get the answers to any questions which remain unanswered. Read it. And give your child a future.

As a parent, your children respect you and want to please you. Encourage them. Help them make their dreams come true. Remember, parent involvement is the most important factor in determining a child's success.

If you have babies, read to them. Answer their questions. Encourage their curiosity and their imagination.

Be positive about school. Children who learn to like school usually find they like to learn.

Once your children begin school, encourage attendance and the completion of homework. Praise even the smallest of their accomplishments. Ask your children to tell you what they learn. Give them time to explain their new thoughts.

Visit the school. Meet the teacher, the counselor. Get involved with the PTA.

Be sure your child takes academic courses—math, science, English, social science, and a foreign language (for example, encourage them to study Spanish).

If your child has been placed in a curriculum that is business or vocational (i.e., not college preparatory), you have the right to have it changed. Demand it.

Prefacio Para Los Padres

La juventud es la esperanza de nuestra sociedad. En ella reside la posibilidad de conseguir un futuro mejor para todos. Por eso, nuestro jovenes necesitan la oportunidad de prepararse bien para cumplir con sus responsibilidades; necesitan más educación, una educación universitaria o un programa de estudios técnicos.

Tal vez su hijo(a) piense trabajar inmediatamente después de terminar sus estudios secundarios. Quizás sea realmente necesario que trabaje para ayudar con los gastos familiares. Pero a largo plazo, el trabajar no es el mejor paso ni para su hijo(a) ni para su familia.

A medida que avanza la tecnología, disminuye la posibilidad de obtener trabajo para los obreros sin entrenamiento adecuado. Para un(a) joven sin educación universitaria o estudios técnicos, a menudo sólo hay trabajos que pagan poco y que no tienen posibilidades de ascenso. La educación universitaria pueda cambiar eso totalmente ya que le da a su hijo(a) la oportunidad de obtener los mejores empleos y asegurarse una posición económica que beneficie tanto a su familia como a su comunidad. Este páis necesita a sus hijos; ellos seran los líderes del futuro: como maestros, doctores, abodgados, comerciantes.

La educación universitaria da a sus hijos la competencia y la confianza necesarias para sobrevivir en el mundo competitivo actual, calificaciones ambas que son tan importantes tanto para su hija como para su hijo. Ésta todavía tiene un papel importante como esposa y madre, función esencial dentro de la familia; pero hoy día este papel se ha complicado porque ella tiene que trabajar para ayudar con los gastos de la casa. La educación universitaria hará posible que su hija contribuya activamente al bienestar de la familia y de la comunidad.

Es importante que ustedes permitan que sus hijos asistan a la universidad, aunque ésta esté lejos de su ciudad o pueblo. No crean que sus hijos estaran solos o sin protección. La universidad tiene habitaciones y planes de comida establecidos, y abundan los servicios y programas de ayuda. La vida en la universidad ayudará a su hijo(a). Allí aprenderá a convivir con otra gente. La experienca universitaria de su hijo(a) también fortalecerá a la familia y a la comunidad. Ninguna universidad quiere que sus estudiantes abandonen sus lazos familiares u olviden su herencia étnica o cultural. De hecho, las universidades quieren que haya diversidad racial y cultural entre sus estudiantes a fin de promover un entendimiento mejor y mayor comprensión entre ellos.

Y no crean ustedes que su familia es demasiado pobre y que, por eso, su hijo(a) no puede asistir a la universidad. El gobierno federal y el gobierno en las diferentes estados tienen dinero para ayudar con los gastos de educación. También las universidades cuentan con fondos de ayuda financiera. Para recibir este dinero hay que completar un formulario de solicitud (Pueden obtener un formulario en las escuela secundaria de su hijo o hija). Si las preguntas parecen un poco complicadas, el (la) consejero(a) de su hijo(a) podrá ayudarlos. Recuerden que es preciso completar ese formulario correctamente para obtener el dinero. El costo de la enseñanza universitaria es muy alto y la mayoría de la gente no puede pagar sin este tipo de ayuda. El dinero existe y está allí para beneficio de sus hijos; El futuro de este país depende en gran parte de la educación de los jovenes. *No tengan ninguna vergüenza en aceptarlo.*

Este folleto explicará en detalle lo relacionado con el proceso de ingreso a la universidad y con la manera de obtener la ayuda económica necesaria. También discutirá otros aspectos de interés y les indicará dónde pueden obtener más información. Léanlo cuidadosamente y den a su hijo(a) la posibilidad de prepararse bien para su vida.

Los hijos respetan a sus padres y quieren satisfacerlos. Los padres deben guiar y aconsejar a sus hijos. Ayúdenlos a que sus sueños se hagan realidad.

Si tienen ninos aún pequeños, contesten sus preguntas y estimulen su curiosidad y su imaginacion.

Cuando su(s) hijo(s) comience(n) la escuela, asegúrense de que asista(n) regularmente a clase y que complete(n) sus tareas. Visiten la escuela y traten de conocer a su(s) maestro(s) y consejero(s). Asegúrense de que su hijo(a) siga cursos académicos: matemáticas, ciencias, inglés, historia, y alguna lengua extranjera (español, si es posible).

Si su hijo(a) ha sido colocad(a) en un programa vocacional o de negocios (en vez de estar en un programa de preparación para la universidad), ustedes, como padres, tienen todo el derecho de pedir un cambio. Si así los quisieran, exijan el cambio lo antes posible.

Chapter 1
Martin Luther King, Jr.,
Jesse Jackson,
Charlotte Wilhite and You

When you are young, you may be judged by your clothes, by your music, by your haircut and by how you talk.

But think about the older people who have really earned your respect, and why. Is it because of the way they look, or is it because of all the good things they have done for our society? Of course, there is Martin Luther King, Jr., but what about Matthew Henson, the black member of Admiral Perry's expedition who in 1909 planted the American flag at the North Pole. He was originally hired as Perry's valet, but proved his abilities as a navigator and arctic expert, and is now buried next to Perry in Arlington National Cemetery. And Phyllis Wheatley, a slave who in 1773 became the second woman to have a book published in the United States, "Poems on Various Subjects, Religious, and Moral." At the age of eighteen, she had to defend her work to a large group of white men in Boston to prove she was indeed the author of the book.

Or Daniel Hale Williams, who in 1893 performed the first successful heart operation; Lewis Latimer, an inventor and engineer who worked with Alexander Graham Bell in developing the first telephone; Booker T. Washington, the founder of Tuskegee University; George Washington Carver, a noted agricultural chemist most famous for developing over 300 products from the peanut (for example, peanut butter), and Thurgood Marshall, one of our greatest and most respected Supreme Court Justices.

The list goes on. Today, Jesse Jackson is the influential leader of the Rainbow Coalition and has been a serious contender for the US Presidency. Doug Wilder was Governor of Virginia. Toni Morrison and August Wilson are both Pulitzer Prize winning authors. Jocelyn Elders is the US Surgeon General. William Raspberry and Carl Rowan are nationally syndicated, influential newspaper columnists. Ben Nighthorse Campbell is a US Senator from Colorado. Carol Mosely Braun is a US Senator from Illinois. Kurt Schmoke is Mayor of Baltimore. Dennis Archer is Mayor of Detroit. Ron Brown unified and turned the Democratic Party around during his tenure as Chair of the Democratic National Committee. He now serves as Secretary of Commerce. Mike Espy is Secretary of Agriculture.

Henry Cisneros is the former Mayor of San Antonio, and the current Secretary of Housing and Urban Development. Colin Powell was Chairman of the Joint Chiefs of Staff, and many people feel, could be the first African-American to win the Presidency. These are some of the most influential people in the United States. They are men and women who overcame great obstacles to earn the respect of the entire nation. You, too, can earn this respect by being:

- The scientist who finds a cure for cancer.
- The lawyer who defends the community.
- The coach who trains the winners.
- The architect who builds the city.
- The teacher who challenges students.
- The citizen who cares about the city and its residents.
- The parent who raises responsible children and provides for their future.

You can be any of these people. Or an author, dentist, newscaster, computer programmer, accountant, pilot, librarian, engineer, or whatever else you want to be or dare to be.

It's your decision. But it's a decision you can't put off any longer. You must make it now, and make it by *setting your sights on a college education.* Education helps people control their own futures and their own dreams. Education is the most important route toward economic independence and self-respect. Remember, only when you respect what you've done with your own life can you gain the respect of others.

Hundreds of thousands of people just like you achieve the goal of a college degree every year. Will the path through college be easy? Maybe yes. Probably no. Nothing worth doing is ever easy. Otherwise, everybody would be an astronaut or lawyer or doctor or engineer...You will be the one who determines how light or how heavy the load. *You and no one else!*

But cheer up. While the decision is yours alone, there is support and there is help. Turn to your parents, counselors, teachers, friends, and employers. Tell them your plans, share your dreams. *Remember: A long trip is always more fun when others go with you.*

You probably didn't get an early start on college planning. You hadn't thought about the future. It didn't seem important. But it's not too late. It never is. Set goals for yourself. Don't be ashamed of working hard. In fact, you might discover that learning isn't as hard as you think!

Now, while you are thinking about it and questioning yourself, take the time to read on and learn how other young people took the first step toward a college education. First meet Charlotte Wilhite. When she wrote this, she was a sophomore at Wayne State University in Detroit.

"An education is not merely a functional system of becoming middle class, but an education makes one self-conscious, self-sufficient, and powerful...An educated person can throw off the belief that he or she is a victim of a maze of uncontrollable forces."

Now meet Rev. Jim Holley from Detroit.

"We've got to go from books to bucks to the ballot...it's all about delivering our people, not only from a spiritual standpoint, but also from an economic standpoint."

Listen to Charlotte Wilhite and Rev. Holley. Read this booklet. Follow its advice. It will help you get started on the road to achievement.

Chapter 2
Meet Some Young People Who Made It—You Can, Too!

You heard Charlotte Wilhite.

Now meet some other young people. See where they came from, where they are now, and how they got there. Their stories appear on the front pages of newspapers every week. They are kids who have survived some very tough neighborhoods, determined to overcome poverty, not only the poverty of material comforts; but perhaps even more crippling, the poverty of opportunities and of hope. As you read their stories, you'll notice some common themes. Most importantly, they were all determined to succeed, despite difficult lives and pressures from other students. Also, most had some help—either a parent or teacher or counselor who understood what they were facing at home and from their classmates. These mentors encouraged them when they started to falter and wonder whether all the work was worth it.

James Monroe High School, New York, NY

Last winter, the *New York Times* profiled a student from James Monroe High School in the South Bronx who's now enrolled at Harvard. The student, like his two sisters before him, had been on course to drop out of high school until a ninth grade algebra teacher started encouraging his interest in schoolwork and his faith in himself. He tells of the pressure he received from his classmates "They would say 'you trying to be white, or what?'" But he kept studying, and slowly, some of them started to compete, and even celebrate if they received a higher grade than him. He was also fortunate to discover the "Bridge to Medicine" program at City College where he received extra tutoring and help with his college applications. "I didn't know about the SAT until 11th grade. Most of us in the Bronx have never heard of the SAT. And it's not our fault." His road has not been easy, and its been pretty solitary. Even at Harvard, he's a bit alone. "The black and Latino students I see are not like me. They almost all come from prep schools or the suburbs." But when asked if he'd go to a different high school if he could do it all over, he replied, "A lot of who

I am today is because of Monroe. As crazy as it sounds, I would probably go to Monroe again!"

Frank Ballou Senior High School, Washington, DC

The Wall Street Journal recently profiled several of the honors students at Frank Ballou Senior High School in Washington DC and their struggle to achieve while being ridiculed by their peers. Being openly smart made them a target. Most of them had few friends, they ate lunch in a classroom rather than risk threats in the cafeteria, and skipped assemblies at which academic honors were handed out to avoid the sneers and jeers of their classmates. Again, the feeling is pervasive. One gang leader remarks, "Everyone knows they're trying to be white, get ahead in a white man's world." Yet a few will overcome the taunts. One student, for instance, had the support of his mother, who devoted herself to keeping her son on the straight and narrow path (while his father sits in jail for armed robbery). He also has the support of his chemistry teacher. When he finally gets his acceptance letter from MIT, he holds it close to his chest and cries, "This is it. My life is about to begin."

Robeson High School, Chicago, IL

One girl at Robeson High School in Chicago was obsessed with college as the ticket to the success she knew she was destined to have. She had no patience for her classmates who had babies, "I'm not going to be another sister out here struggling, knocked up with two or three babies, on aid and the father's out there with somebody else." She carried her college acceptance letter around with her for weeks!

Another student talked of being late for school because it took "extra time to heat the bath water on a hot plate." "If I get killed, I just get killed. I wasn't going to let it keep me from coming to school." This student was described as a nice boy who never gets a break. He keeps to himself and says he has no role models. In fact, he confides only to his journal, "It's like having a broken step on your stairs and having the tools to fix it but not fixing it 'cause you're scared you will hurt your finger or something."

William Jackson, Engineer

Finally, here's a letter from William Jackson, a successful young black engineer:

Mr. Jackson writes to you:
"A lot of young people are bitter, as I was, and this poison is a product of their environment and lack of self-esteem. I say to you, 'Admit that you

12

are angry with yourself. You want to change. And you're going to make the investment of time, energy, and faith in yourself to overcome the barriers that stand in your way. Believe in yourself!'

"I know you are searching, or else you wouldn't be reading my words. Today I am a successful engineer. I have my story. Now tell your story through your actions. Listen to those who can help you and keep your mind open as you prepare for college and your trip to self-esteem, growth and success.

"God Bless You."

William Jackson

Chapter 3
Good Reasons for Going to College

YOU STILL HAVE CHOICES

When you are young, you still have choices—choices that will determine what kind of life you will lead.

It can be a good life—one that sets your spirit free and turns dreams into reality.

Or it can be a frustrating life—one that leaves you to drift, powerless to control even your own destiny.

Make the right choice now. You still have the luxury of time; but time, once emptied, cannot be refilled like the gas tank of a car. Or, more poetically put:

Nothing can bring back the hour
Of splendor in the grass, of glory in the flower.

—William Wordsworth

Now is the time—the right time—to prepare yourself for the adult roles you can assume, that are your right to assume, and that society wants you to assume.

It is your life. Begin it with a college education. The rewards are guaranteed to be as abundant as the challenges.

WHAT COLLEGE DOES FOR YOU

In simplest terms, you can expect two things from your college experience—developed personal skills, and the core knowledge of an academic field, such as education or engineering. There is no wall between personal skills and occupational knowledge. They interact to bring you personal satisfaction and the self-confidence necessary to become a respected and contributing member of the community.

PERSONAL SKILLS

Personal skills are those that allow the mind to be free, which in turn allow the person to be free. They are developed through literacy and a liberal education. Personal skills include:

- Learning to learn.
- Learning to write and speak effectively.
- Learning to listen with care.
- Learning to analyze a problem.
- Learning to persuade others to your point of view.
- Learning to help others overcome problems.
- Learning to work with people from all backgrounds.
- Learning to set goals.
- Learning to manage time effectively.
- Learning to demonstrate initiative, make decisions.
- Learning to accept responsibility.
- Learning to deal with change.

OCCUPATIONAL KNOWLEDGE

A professional field, whether it is accounting, forestry, business, law, literature, or medicine, is a specialized body of knowledge. That knowledge is acquired in a college classroom. The college degree is the passport that permits entrance to the professional fields. Without the degree, the doors to the professional fields are closed to you forever.

You may ask, "but I don't know what I want to be. Shouldn't I decide before I go off to college?" That would be a serious mistake. You don't need a career goal to enter college. You don't even need to have a specific academic interest. In fact, once in college, you will have one or two years or even longer to test, to explore, to settle on a direction.

Remember, no matter which professional path you ultimately follow, you have to start with the freshman year of college.

As further encouragement, here is a list of ten of the top growing occupational fields of the next ten years—all of which require two to four years of college:

- Computer Science: systems analysts, programmers, technicians.
- Health: nurses, doctors, dieticians, administrators.
- Engineering: mechanical, electrical, nuclear, civil.
- Teaching: kindergarten, elementary, science and math.

- Money Management: accountants, bankers.
- Therapists: occupational, physical, respiratory.
- Law: lawyers, legal assistants, paralegals.
- Resource Management
- Planning: Architects, surveyors.
- Social Services: Psychologists, consumer advocates.

The nation's need for well-educated people will continue long into the future. As we approach the year 2000, and technology continues to advance, manufacturing companies will require fewer and fewer people to operate equipment, while jobs in service industries are flourishing. This means most of the low-skill jobs will soon be gone and employers will be more desperate than ever to hire educated people. In fact, if more people do not become educated, many jobs will go unfilled, and our nation's ability to compete in a worldwide marketplace will be severely diminished. After all, a nation's most valuable resource is the minds of its people. And as the columnist Richard Cohen points out, that's the best kind of resource to rely on—it's renewable and can never be depleted unless we allow it to be.

INTERACTION OF PERSONAL SKILLS AND OCCUPATIONAL KNOWLEDGE

How important is the interaction of personal skills and occupational knowledge? Ask yourself the following questions.

- Could you be a scientist without knowing how to gather information?
- Could you be an executive without knowing how to handle responsibility?
- Could you be a computer programmer without knowing how to analyze and solve a problem?
- Could you be a supervisor without knowing how to listen and see all sides of an issue?
- Could you be a lawyer without being able to speak articulately and persuasively?

Highly developed personal skills will allow you to succeed in whatever career field you choose. They will also provide you with long-term economic independence; the flexibility to move quickly, even from one career to another if the field you have chosen turns out to be less fulfilling or challenging or rewarding than you thought. Maybe technological change is smothering the opportunities in your field. Your personal skills will flash you the warning signs, well in advance, and help you identify new opportunities. Personal skills will be your insurance for a rewarding life.

Personal skills will also allow you to advance in whatever career field you choose. The higher you rise, the more important these skills become. The top people in any organization accomplish their goals by working through people, not through things. They function by leading, by motivating, and by persuading.

WHAT ABOUT EARNINGS?

College graduates earn more. That's a fact. We could publish long tables here, developed by the Census Bureau, that list lifetime earnings of high school dropouts, high school graduates, and college graduates, by age, by sex, by race.

But why waste time with tables? They show but two things. First, that the employment rate of college graduates is much higher than the employment rate of high school graduates (7% higher for men; 13% higher for women). And second, that the salary of people with a college degree ($2,116 per month) is nearly twice that of people with only a high school diploma ($1,077 per month), and four times that of people who dropped out of high school ($492 per month). If you extend this difference (including annual raises) over a forty-year career, a college graduate will earn nearly $1.5 million more than someone whose education stopped with high school.

That $1.5 million will purchase a better home, nicer furniture, nicer cars, vacations, tickets to concerts and athletic events, improved medical care, and, an education for your children.

OBSTACLES

We have made the case for college. We hope you are convinced. But being convinced and doing something about it may not be the same thing. You are probably thinking about obstacles now and, in your mind, these obstacles are higher and steeper than you can handle.

Not so.

Some of the obstacles exist only in your head. They include false beliefs and misconceptions about how hard it is to get into college and how there is no money to pay for it once you're there.

Some of the obstacles are caused by confusion about how to pick a college and apply for admission; what tests to take; what forms to fill out; when to do all these things and in what order. This is easily cleared up.

Some of the obstacles arise because you had not thought much about college until your senior year and therefore you didn't take some of the preparatory courses in your sophomore and junior years. These obstacles are real and we recognize that. But, at the same time, it is never too late. You may have lost some options, but plenty of others remain. There are special strategies for those who wait until the last second, strategies that will help you skirt the obstacles. The remainder of this booklet will:

- Clear your mind of false beliefs.
- Give you admissions and financial aid know-how; where to look and how to apply.
- Outline special strategies for the late bloomers.
- Present a time table to keep you on track.

**We know you can do it.
So, read, learn, then do!**

Chapter 4
Some Things You Believe About College Just Aren't So

You have to get rid of false beliefs about college. Too many students have walked into a cage of false beliefs, snapped shut the lock, and now can't get out.

How do we know about these false beliefs? Mrs. Slocum, Ms. Leider and Mr. Leider visited high schools in Chicago, Detroit, Los Angeles, New York City, and Washington, D.C., to meet with hundreds of students and their counselors.

Typical questions we asked: Are you planning to go to college? Which college? Why that college and not another? Does college scare you? Why don't you want to go to college? Do you think you can handle college work? Why or why not?

Some of the answers were inspirational. They left Mrs. Slocum and the Leiders feeling good about meeting so many sincere and earnest young people who wanted to improve themselves.

But some of the answers raised concern. They showed there were some students who could not move forward. They were blocked by obstacles they had constructed themselves.

The questions and answers that follow will help you to re-examine your priorities and overcome many of these false beliefs.

 ## Priority #1
"I want to start earning money now..."

Student

Sure, I know about college. I have thought about it. But right now it's more important for me to find a job after graduating from high school and earn some real money. I don't want to wait any longer.

Mrs. Slocum

You probably won't have any trouble finding a low-skill job like working in a warehouse or a fast food restaurant. And after you start work, you will make some money, certainly more than you make now.

But what about your future? The jobs you are talking about don't lead anywhere. Ten years from now, you will still be working in a warehouse or a fast food restaurant. And your take-home pay will not be much more than when you started. If you grumble about your pay, the boss can easily replace you with a younger person who is just starting out and who will work for less.

And if you quit, you are not likely to find another job. By the year 2000, three out of four jobs will require some education or technical training beyond high school. The skills needed by employers will be the skills you develop in college—reading, writing, math, speaking, listening, reasoning, and using computers.

Your decision would make sense if that low-paying job was not going to be your lifetime occupation but a stop-out for a year or two, while you earn some money for college. Also, a job can nourish self-esteem and teach you responsibility to others, punctuality and discipline. But there are risks.

It is not easy to go back to study habits after a long interruption. Also, you could pick up responsibilities, such as a husband or wife or baby, that may prevent you from returning to school. These kinds of responsibilities can easily lock you into that dead-end job.

My advice: It's best to go straight on to college, without any detours. Then, in four years, you will reap the bigger rewards of a college education. Be patient...

 ## Priority #2
"I've saved up some money. I sure want to buy a car..."

Student

I've saved a couple of thousand dollars from part-time jobs. I really want this car and I can get a good deal buying it. I can do a lot with a car.

Mrs. Slocum

I agree that you can do a lot with a car. But you can do even more with an education. A car will move you over a road. An education will move you through life. By choosing a short ride down the strip, you might forsake the big ride to a big future.

That's philosophy. But if philosophy doesn't grab you, try some numbers.

Say you have saved $5,000 and use it to buy a car. What will the car be worth four years from now? $1,500?

Now invest that same $5,000 in a college education. What will that be worth four years from now? $1.5 million in higher lifetime earnings.

So what will it be? $1,500 or $1.5 million?

||| Priority #3
||| "My friends all talk about joining the Army."

Student

I really don't know what to do after high school. If I join the military, I'll at least be guaranteed a job.

Ms. Leider

A career in the military is not for everyone. At a minimum, those who enlist in the uniformed services are required to get a haircut, do some push-ups, obey all orders, and salute superior officers. Discipline is very strict. Drugs are not tolerated. Before you enlist, talk to people already in the service, not just the recruiters.

If serving your nation in this way still appeals to you, make certain you take advantage of the military's generous education benefits. Here's how. Go on active duty for four years. While on active duty, take off-duty courses (for which the military will pay 75% of the tuition costs) and make sure the courses add up to an associate's degree. At the same time, participate in the Montgomery GI Bill. For every dollar you put in (up to $1,200), Uncle Sam will contribute eight (up to a maximum of $9,600). When your enlistment is over, you will have credit for two years of college, and a tuition kitty of at least $10,800 to help you pay for your last two years of college.

If you decide to stay in the military, sign up for the reserves while you're in college and go to Officer Candidate School when you graduate. Then, when you're ready to begin your military career, you'll be an officer, making more money than enlisted personnel with even more years in service.

||| False Belief #1
||| "I can't afford college..."

Student

I do want to go to college. But who will pay for it? My family can't afford it and there is so little financial aid...

Mr. Leider

Think again. In the coming school year, there will be nearly $40 billion in student aid—in scholarships, grants, work, and loan opportunities. Uncle Sam is again becoming generous with this money because he finally realizes it will reduce the $100 billion he spends each year on programs like welfare, unemployment, and prisons.

The trick in getting financial aid is in applying—that is, in applying correctly and in applying in advance of the deadlines. Read Chapter 6 with great care. It will teach you all the ins and outs of student aid.

But to put your fears at rest right now, I asked a number of financial aid officers to tell me how a student, whose family has no money whatever, can finance an education either at an expensive private college or at a less expensive state university. Their answer: It can be done through a combination of scholarships, work opportunities, and loans. These examples use estimated 1995/96 data:

DAVIDSON COLLEGE, Davidson, NC
Annual Cost: $25,750

Pell Grant	$ 2,300
Supplemental Educational Opportunity Grant	$ 2,000
Institutional Scholarships/Grants	$11,450
Loans/Campus Work	$10,000
TOTAL AID	$25,750

HAVERFORD COLLEGE, Haverford, PA
Annual Cost: $29,200

Pell Grant	$ 2,300
Supplemental Educational Opportunity Grant	$ 2,900
Institutional Scholarships/Grants	$15,000
Loan	$ 7,500
Campus Job	$ 1,500
TOTAL AID	$29,200

STATE UNIVERSITY OF NEW YORK AT ALBANY
Annual Cost (State Resident): $9,400

Pell Grant	$ 2,300
Supplemental Educational Opportunity Grant	$ 2,400
NY State Grant	$ 2,200
Loan	$ 2,500
TOTAL AID	$ 9,400

RUTGERS UNIVERSITY, New Brunswick, NJ
Annual Cost (State Resident): $10,900

Pell Grant	$ 2,300
NJ Tuition Aid Grant	$ 1,400
Educational Opportunity Fund	$ 1,200
Supplemental Educational Opportunity Grant	$ 2,000
Perkins Loan/Stafford Loan	$ 4,000
TOTAL AID	$10,900

SPELMAN COLLEGE, Atlanta, Georgia
Annual Cost:: $17,900

Pell Grant	$ 2,300
State Scholarship	$ 4,000
University Grant	$ 3,000
Perkins Loan/Stafford Loan	$ 5,100
Work Study	$ 1,500
Private Scholarship	$ 2,000
TOTAL AID	$17,900

I could give more examples. From schools in the Midwest and in the South. Public and private. From other historically black colleges. But I think I made the point. Aid is available.

There is, however, one troublesome area in the sample aid packages—and you probably noted it, too. The amount of money available for grants and scholarships no longer comes close to covering college costs, so schools are having to make loans a much larger part of every package. And that brings us to the next false belief: a mortal fear of loans.

 ## False Belief #2
"I don't want to go in debt to get educated..."

Student
There may be aid, but most of it is in loans. I am scared to death of loans. What happens if I can't find a job after graduation? How can I pay it back then? And what will they do to me if I don't pay it back?

Mr. Leider

Relax. Student loans have three key features that keep them from being scary.

1. You don't pay anything on your loan—principal or interest—until six (or nine) months after you have completed your studies. That gives you at least half a year to find a job and begin earning good money.
2. Inflation and pay raises work in your favor. As the years pass, your monthly loan repayments take smaller and smaller bites from your paycheck. That needs explaining. Say, you must repay your loan at the rate of $100 per month for ten years. In the first year, $100 may represent more than a day's pay. But five years from now, because of inflation and your now higher salary, $100 becomes a half a day's pay. And ten years from now, $100 shrinks to two hours of work.
3. And if you can't find a job, you are still protected. You ask the lender for "forbearance." Forbearance means permission to (1) temporarily stop making payments or (2) extend the time for making payments or (3) make smaller payments than were scheduled. Typical reasons for forbearance include unemployment, poor health, and serious personal problems.

Remember, long-term loans work in your favor. That's how you can finance a home, a business, an education—even a summer vacation. It's a technique based on confidence in yourself and in your future. It's a technique you must learn to adopt.

 ## False Belief #3
"The local college may not be the best school, but at least it's close to home and I can afford it..."

Student

I can probably get a better education at another college. But if I enroll at my local college, I can live at home, continue to help look after my family, and save on room and board. That leaves tuition, and my mother thinks she can swing it.

Mr. Leider

First, you should never assume a college is out of your price range. After all, the whole purpose of financial aid is to equalize educational opportunities. Instead, always begin by picking the schools that are best for you in terms of course offerings, reputation, support programs, and other academic factors. Never start by picking schools on the basis of cost. Remember, if the school wants you, the financial aid office will find a way for you to pay. After you read the chapter on financial aid, you will understand how.

Second, you might be helping your family more by getting the best education you can. Not only will you be able to get a better job, but you'll be a great role model and better able to advise your younger brothers and sisters when it's time for them to think about college.

False Belief #4
"It takes high SAT scores to get into college..."

Student

I've heard you need high SAT scores to get into college. I haven't taken the SAT. But I know if I do, I won't score high enough to win admission...

Mr. Leider

Let's talk honestly about the SAT, and when I say SAT, I also mean the ACT—the admission test produced by the American College Testing Program and used in the Midwest and the South.

Over the past few years, the SAT has been severely criticized for its role in college admissions. It doesn't measure intelligence, motivation or creativity, so it cannot possibly predict academic success. To deflect some of this criticism, the College Board changed the name of the test from "Scholastic *Aptitude* Test" to "Scholastic *Assessment* Test," and introduced minor changes in the test's format. The College Board announced these changes with great hoopla sending even the most prepared students into a tail spin (and tripling enrollment in test prep classes). The College Board insists the New SAT places a greater focus on testing students reasoning and critical thinking skills, but this new claim is a stretch. The only thing SAT scores seem to do (reliably) is correspond closely to a family's income—the higher the income, the higher the scores. Fortunately, despite the cosmetic work, the wise people who thought little of the usefulness of the old SAT seem to feel the same way about the new one. (Similarly, the people who thought the old SAT served a beneficial purpose, think the new version will do so as well.)

That's one item of bad news. Now for another one: Many state university systems, like those in Texas and California, relate admissions to a numerical achievement standard based, in part, on the SAT and, in part, on a grade point average in academic subjects. Many private colleges also use SAT scores as admission cut-offs. Such colleges, to demonstrate that they are becoming "more selective," tend to raise the minimum scores required for entry.

So what can you do? As one school superintendent told us, there's no question that standardized tests contain bias. And, the only recourse is to deal with it the way it is. They aren't going to make up a new game for us.

In "dealing with it" there is also some good news. Practicing for the SAT and getting coaching can improve scores. Your school may have a coaching course. If it does, enroll. If you can't find a course in your school, one may be sponsored by a neighborhood group or a church.

In the absence of a coaching course, borrow an SAT preparation book from the library or counseling office and take practice tests. This will build your confidence and sharpen your test taking skills. Be sure you use a current test prep book because the "New SAT" has some format changes and you don't want to practice for sections that have been eliminated. For example, the grammar section (Test of Standard Written English) is gone, so is the antonym section. Also, the reading passages are longer and the Math section requires students to produce their own answers to some of the questions. Finally, student are also now allowed to use calculators.

Above all, don't panic. To the best of my knowledge, no one has ever died taking the SAT.

There is another bit of good news. Most admission officers realize the SAT does not measure cultural intelligence, intuitive intelligence, creative intelligence, or imaginative intelligence. They also understand that the test contains cultural bias. These admission officers look for other qualities in an applicant—determination, the ability to overcome adversity, a drive to succeed, and maturity. These are the characteristics that will allow students to succeed in college, and in the complicated world they must enter upon graduating from college.

I asked a group of these progressive admission officers to draw for this booklet quick portraits of disadvantaged students who were accepted for personal qualities and potential, and not because of their SAT scores. All these students, incidentally, did well in college.

As you read these stories, keep in mind the average SATs last year were 424 (verbal), and 478 (math), the average SATs for black students were 353 (verbal) and 388 (math), and the average SATs for Latino students fell somewhere in between. Also keep in mind, that after April, 1995 the College Board plans to "recenter" SAT scores so the average on both the Math and Verbal sections will be 500 (and score comparisons with the students profiled here will be meaningless).

A LIBERAL ARTS COLLEGE IN PENNSYLVANIA

He was heavily involved in extracurricular activities, serving as president of the Puerto Rican cultural club and as a leader of several community organizations. He impressed us as an all-around student. We felt he was much stronger than his test scores. We decided the low scores reflected his bilingual background so we didn't give them much weight.

A CATHOLIC UNIVERSITY IN CALIFORNIA

Her family lives in a low-income, high minority area where few students graduate from high school and even fewer continue on to college.

She started high school with a heavy load of vocational courses. Eventually, she decided on a future in engineering. This required her to enroll in night courses and summer courses to make up on college preparatory work.

She demonstrated to us her willingness and determination to overcome linguistic and academic deficiencies.

She was granted admittance even though her SATs were a 390 Verbal and 450 Math. We felt this hard-working, self-determined young woman deserved a chance to fulfill her dream.

A LIBERAL ARTS COLLEGE IN VERMONT

Son of separated parents, both unemployed, in a large northeastern city. The family life of this young man is not stable. Example: he went home one day, discovered the family's apartment had burned down and the family had moved and left no forwarding address.

He is the eldest of four children and the first in his family to attend college. His scores were 370 Verbal and 370 Math. However, his interviewer said, "Take him! He is not a 300+ Verbal. He is very articulate and has a solid understanding of his self and the world around him. Confident in the most positive way. He's done a hell of a job considering his background!"

A MIDWESTERN UNIVERSITY

Daughter of a clerk at a steel company. Mother is unemployed. Fourth child in a family of seven. Secretary of senior class. Secretary of French club. Student Council. In her personal statement and essay she wrote about Dr. Martin Luther King and his dream of equality and how she sees some evidence of his dreams becoming reality. Her teacher described her as "intelligent... motivated...responsible...one who goes beyond what is expected or required."

A STATE UNIVERSITY IN THE SOUTH

The personal quality we most admired was her tenacity. This student comes from a foster home. She has maintained a strong academic record while enduring family upheaval and separation from siblings. SAT Verbal was 350...A very mature, articulate and goal-oriented person.

A MIDWESTERN UNIVERSITY

Son of a factory worker. Dropped out of high school his junior year. He began his own reading program at home and took the G.E.D. exam for a high school diploma. SAT scores were 370 Verbal and 430 Math. In his interview he convinced the counselor he had high personal goals and he worked well on his own. A highly motivated and very determined young man.

A PRIVATE UNIVERSITY IN CONNECTICUT

A young man whose mother supports the family as a bookkeeper (his father is unknown). Apparently feeling his SATs were not strong enough, he submitted this bit of poetry for the admission committee's consideration:

I don't wish to be too wordy,
I'm not one to be verbose.
I want to say with candor,
I'm the man who has the most!

I'm intelligent and witty,
Realistic with foresight.
Responsible and pithy,
And if I might say, bright.

But my knowledge stretches past,
The score upon the test.
I'm always learning something,
And my grades will tell the rest.

I have hobbies to involve me,
Such as Art and Architecture.
Rubik's Cube and Crosswords,
In such things I find adventure.

My drive can be contagious,
My devotion quite delightful.
When I'm writing I'm courageous,
But my exaggeration's frightful!

So I can predict a future,
Where opportunities abound.
To develop every talent,
And to make those talents sound.

False Belief #5
"You have to take college prep courses starting in your freshman year of high school if you want to go to college..."

Student

They say I have to have four years of English, four years of math, and three years of science to go to college. Well, I didn't think about college until I started my senior year. There is no way I can make up all these courses in my last year in high school.

Mrs. Slocum

It's never too late. First of all, entrance requirements vary with each institution. A recent study concluded that while many colleges do require a college preparatory program for admission, a surprising number (especially state schools) only recommend one. You still may have to work harder now to make up lost ground—take some night courses and courses next summer. Or you may have to find a college with a strong developmental program (instruction in the academic subjects that you should have taken in high school, but didn't). That shouldn't be too hard since 89.8% of all four-year colleges and universities offer remedial courses. Another option would be to take the first two years of college at a nearby community college or junior college where you can strengthen your academic preparation. Above all, never think it's too late for you to get started. If it's any consolation, over one-quarter of all college freshmen take a remedial math course, 11.8% take a science course, 11.6% take an English course, and 5.2% take a reading course.

Remember, there are many routes that you can follow, regardless of what you have done during your first three years of high school.

False Belief #6
"I may be interested, but I'd like to talk to someone first and I really don't know anybody who has gone to college. Nobody in my family has..."

Student

I have a lot of questions about college. If I can get these questions answered, I might want to go to college. But my mother doesn't know anything about college and my older brother didn't go to college either. He joined the Army.

Mrs. Slocum

It's true. You may think you have no college educated role models. African-Americans and Latinos are greatly underrepresented in business, politics, and leadership positions of all kinds. Remember, however, that every teacher in your high school is a college graduate. Your counselors are college graduates. Members of the clergy are college graduates. Social workers are college graduates. In the clinic, the doctors, nurses and therapists are college graduates. If you walk up to any of these people and say, "I'm interested in going to college, but I have a few questions," nobody will say, "Beat it, I'm too busy." In fact, the people you ask will be flattered, delighted, and helpful. After you break the ice, don't just ask one person. Ask several. Some may favor big schools, others like small schools. Some will say stay close to home, others will suggest you go far away. Listen to all of them and watch your college knowledge grow.

False Belief #7
"I am scared to go off somewhere where I don't know anybody and everybody there is different..."

Student

I know everybody in my neighborhood. My friends are here. We understand each other without saying a word. But the college I am thinking about is a "white school." It scares me...

Mrs. Slocum

Until a few years ago I thought we blacks were the only people who had experienced oppression. But then I took a course in ethnic studies at a local university, and it was an eye opener to learn that other groups—the Irish, Poles, Jews, Indians, Chicanos, Latinos— had suffered like we had and struggled like we had. I discovered bonds I had not thought possible and made many new friends.

But such an understanding takes time. It doesn't come immediately. I know what you are saying, and your concern is a valid one. In reality, it may be difficult to adjust to life at a school that is far away or predominantly white. Keep in mind that all freshmen are lost during the first weeks of school—especially the ones who seem the most self-assured. Initially, however, you may need the special support that only people from your own cultural background can give you. When looking at a college, make it a point to find out whether it sponsors minority organizations, such as an African-American House or a Latino Student Union. Also ask about mentor programs and special fall orientations. Minority organizations do provide the security and strength that come from togetherness. But no matter how much cultural support a college may offer, you're still going to experience some loneliness. Here's one suggestion: Before you leave for college, be sure to pack items that remind you of your family. Photographs are especially reassuring.

Chapter 5
What You Need to Know About College Selection & Admission

Buying a car is a lot easier than picking a college. There are no more than a hundred different models from which to choose. You can test drive before making a final choice. And there is plenty of consumer advice around to balance the hype from the automobile manufacturers—advice on fuel consumption, repair frequency, safety features, warranties, and trade-in values.

But when you turn to college, you don't deal with a mere hundred choices. It's like facing a showroom with over 3,000 models. Only you can't try any of them out with a test enrollment, and consumer information is hard to find. Almost all college admission information is slanted as it is prepared by the colleges themselves. This information comes in all forms—fliers, posters, brochures, handbooks, catalogues, and laser disk presentations. One hardly knows where to start or what to believe.

Some colleges have familiar names. You know them because of the fame of their graduates or the power of their athletic teams. Others you know about because they are in your town or your state.

But most of the names will be new to you. What's behind these names? All kinds of schools. Big schools and small schools. Schools that are state or city operated and schools that are privately operated. Many schools were founded by religious groups while others have no religious affiliation. In some schools, minorities are the majority. In most, minorities are represented in a much smaller percentage than in the population as a whole. Some are two-year colleges. Some are four-year colleges. Some award graduate and professional degrees. Some schools are in urban settings, some are in the suburbs, and some are in rural areas. Many schools are in warm climates and others are where the winters are long and cold. A few schools are extremely selective, accepting no more than one of every ten applicants. Others have open admission and accept all who apply. Some have rigorous application deadlines; miss one and you needn't bother to fill out the forms. Others use "rolling admission" where soon as your application is processed. Some schools are good in every department. Some have strong and weak departments. Sports are important in some colleges, business is more important in others. Some schools encourage fraternities and sororities. Others prohibit them. Some schools have only male students. Others accept only women. Most are co-ed.

Choices present problems for everyone. Making a choice becomes especially difficult if you have waited until your senior year to begin thinking about where you want to go. For many people, the process begins at a very early age. Mom and dad have been arguing about the "right college" ever since their child entered kindergarten. They themselves are usually college graduates. Their friends and relatives are college graduates. They have been buying books on college preparation and college selection. And, by the time their child enters high school, the choice of colleges has been narrowed to six or seven.

But what about you? Your parents may not have gone to college. There are probably no books at home about college preparation and college selection. You aren't able to drive around the countryside, visiting seven schools in seven states to find the one school just right for you. On some days, you don't even have the bus fare to check out Downtown University.

So what can you do? Three things. One—become even more resolute in your drive to go on. Two—take the crash course on college selection and admission which comes next in this chapter. And—three—after reading this chapter, apply the "shortcut strategies" most appropriate to you. This will help you pick the handful of colleges best suited to your needs from the three thousand choices available.

CRASH COURSE: HOW HARD IS IT TO GET IN?

Look at following chart.

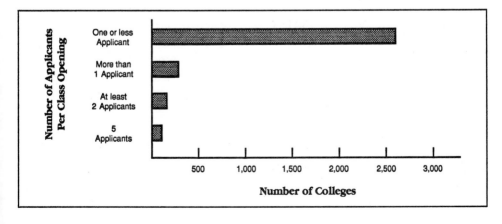

Few colleges have more than one applicant for each class opening. Most don't have enough applicants. In fact, 91.3% of all students get into their first or second choice school.

Of those that can pick and choose, a handful gets as many as five highly qualified applicants for each spot in the freshman class. Some 40 or 50 receive at least two applicants. Another 300 don't get two applicants, but they get enough applicants to reject some potential students who meet all entrance requirements.

The remaining 2600+ schools have more classroom spaces than applicants. That, however, should not lead you into thinking you can get in, merely by paying an application fee. Most of these schools do have admission requirements which they spell out in their catalogues and many will turn away students who don't meet these requirements. Usually, they have three requirements:

One—the applicant must be a high school graduate.

Two—the applicant must have completed from 11 to 16 college preparatory units (also known as Carnegie Units). These may include four years (units) of high school English, two or three years (units) of mathematics, and the rest of the units in foreign languages, social sciences, and the physical sciences (Remember to check with the school to find out if these units are required or recommended).

Three—the applicant must achieve a satisfactory score on one of two college aptitude tests—the ACT or the SAT.

As a general rule, these are the admission requirements you will encounter:

HIGHLY SELECTIVE. Two or more applicants for each vacancy.
- HS Graduation
- High Class Standing
- High Grade Point Average in College Preparatory Courses
- High ACT/SAT Scores
- 3 Achievement Tests (tests which measure mastery of a subject)
- 16 College Preparatory Units
- Essay (which allows you to express your life goals)
- Interview (can be conducted in your home town)
- 2 or More Recommendations
- Community Service
- Early Application Deadline—Often sometime in January

COMPETITIVE. More than one but less than two applicants for each vacancy.
- HS Graduation
- High Class Standing

- High Grade Point Average in College Preparatory Courses
- High ACT/SAT Scores
- 14 College Preparatory Units
- Interview Recommended, Not Required
- 2 or More Recommendations
- Early Application Deadline—Often February

AVERAGE. Fewer applicants than vacancies but schools adhere to admission requirements.
- HS Graduation
- Average Class Standing or Better
- Passing Grades—Cs and Bs
- Median ACT/SAT Scores
- 11 to 14 College Preparatory Units
- Recommendations Considered
- Later Application Deadline—Could Extend to May or June

OPEN ADMISSIONS. Accept all qualified students.
- HS Graduation or equivalent (GED Test)
- College Will Test Applicant for Placement

Don't let these tables intimidate you into applying only to the schools with the least demanding admission requirements.

Some schools, as you will recall from the "SAT" discussion in the last chapter, are indeed unbending in their standards. But many more are flexible. They will insist you meet all their admission requirements, but your performance under each requirement is subject to an evaluation. In other words, if these schools say, "Take the SAT," you take the SAT. By not taking the test, you disqualify yourself from admission. But taking the test and not doing well does not necessarily mean rejection.

Most schools, as you will recall from the "College Prep" discussion in the last chapter, offer remedial courses in math, reading, and writing. While these courses do not usually count toward fulfilling your degree requirements, some schools will accept you as a "special student." In other words, you can be admitted without the necessary College Preparatory Units provided you pass proficiency tests or enroll in the necessary remedial courses.

The admission officers at these schools—and they include public and private colleges—recognize that minority students achieve under much more difficult circumstances than white, middle class students. You may not have been challenged. You may not have had the home support that builds self-esteem. You may not have been taught well. You may have experienced negative pressure from your peers. And you may have experienced problems with the cultural bias of standardized tests.

If you're the first in your family to go to college, make sure the admission directors know. Because of the barriers you face, and have overcome, you are probably going to do much better in college than your record indicates, and they know that.

In your case, progressive admission officers will look for indicators other than the traditional yardsticks of class standing, grade point average, and ACT/SAT scores. They will look for drive and determination, tenacity and a desire to succeed, leadership and a sense of responsibility. These characteristics, not high test scores, will make you successful and respected.

For this reason we say: Aim high on the collegiate selectivity ladder. Don't automatically head for the bottom.

Prepare for all the admission requirements. If they call for a test, register for the test. If they call for an interview, request an interview. If they call for recommendations, arrange for recommendations. If they call for an essay, start writing. But PREPARE.

And then apply.

CRASH COURSE CONTINUED: HOW MANY APPLICATIONS?

Smart gamblers hedge their bets. That gives them protection. They may not win as much; but at the same time, they limit their losses. No matter what happens, they don't get wiped out.

Smart college picking works the same way. You can't be sure your first choice school will take you. And the fact that your application may be based on drive and personality rather than on high academic achievement and test scores adds to the uncertainty.

So what do you do? You also hedge. How? By applying to more than one school.

Here is what we suggest:

- Pick one or two schools where your chances of getting in are slim.
- Pick one or two schools where you have a fifty-fifty chance.
- Pick one school where the odds of admission are in your favor.
- Pick one school where you know for sure you'll be accepted.

Apply to all of these schools. You may get accepted by the most selective school on your list. Or you may not. But you will get accepted somewhere, and that's what is important.

What about the rejections you pick up? Should you take these personally? Do you consider them as a blow to your ego? Of course not. Let's go back to the gambler. If he loses, do you think he develops doubts about his own judgment and tears his hair out? No. He recognizes that it's a game; and in any game there must be winners and losers; and today's losers may be tomorrow's winners. He sees nothing personal in the turn of events. You shouldn't either.

Admittedly, no one likes to be rejected. In a perverse way, however, anger you might feel at rejection is healthy. It means you think enough of yourself and your abilities that you resent someone who tells you "no." Having said all this, I want to emphasize again—rejection by a college, especially one of the so-called "prestige" colleges, should not be viewed as a failure. It doesn't matter what school name is on your diploma; if you have character, creativity, and industry, you will succeed. Still have doubts? Think about this: The word "prestige" is derived from the Latin word "praestigium" which means illusion, delusion, or juggler's trick.

CRASH COURSE CONTINUED: SHOULD I WORRY ABOUT COLLEGE COSTS?

Not at this time. Financial aid is available to cover most college expenses as long as you apply correctly, to the right agencies, and in advance of the deadlines.

Your greatest problem, at this time, may be with fees—something we have not yet talked about. You will find there are fees for taking the ACT and the SAT. Fees for college applications. Fees, later on, for filing your financial aid application. Besides these fees, there are additional costs. The cost of envelopes and stationery. The cost of making copies of all your applications. The cost of postage stamps.

You can request fee waivers. But these waivers won't cover everything. If you apply to several colleges—and you should—you may need as much as one hundred to three hundred dollars over a four month period, from September through January. That is a lot. We know it. We have a few suggestions that may help, and we'll share these with you in Chapter 8.

CRASH COURSE CONTINUED: IT'S IMPORTANT TO BE ORGANIZED

You must make every day count in the first semester of your senior year in high school. You will be "preparing" and "applying."

Preparing includes:
- Signing up for the right courses.
- Sharing your college plans with teachers and counselors.
- Registering for the tests you must take, building self-confidence for the tests, and then taking the tests.

- Identifying the teachers and counselors who will write your letters of recommendation.

Applying includes:
- Gathering information about colleges.
- Identifying the schools that interest you.
- Filling out and mailing off the college application and financial aid application forms.

Chapter 7 contains a timetable that will help you organize your senior year. The back of this book includes some worksheets to help you organize the college selection and application process.

YOU'LL HAVE TO TAKE SOME SHORT CUTS

Ok, you say. I understand that time is short. I have lots to do. How can I quickly narrow down that list of 3000 plus schools to the six or seven that may be the best for me and my life goals?

The answer: You'll have to take some short cuts.

SHORT CUT STRATEGY: SOURCES OF COLLEGE INFORMATION

Where does one get information about colleges? Generally, there are six sources.

1. **People who Have Been To College**—teachers, counselors, ministers, religious leaders. Stay a moment after class to talk to a favorite teacher. Make an appointment with a counselor or minister. Tell them you want to go to college and ask for their recommendations.

   Before giving you a recommendation, teachers and counselors will probably want to know if you have made career plans, check into your course load and grades, ask about your preferences such as large schools or small schools, distant schools or close-by schools. Then they will give you their ideas. They may also suggest their own college. Have a pencil and piece of paper handy and take down their recommendations.

2. **College Directories.** College directories are of two types. Some directories record what the colleges say about themselves and others record what outside observers say about the colleges.

   Examples of the first kind are the College Board's *College Handbook*, Lovejoy's *College Guide*, and Arco's *The Right College*.

This kind of directory can come in book form or as a computer program.

The second kind of directory contains opinions about the colleges. It is important to remember that these are only opinions. Included here are Cass and Birnbaum's *Comparative Guide to American Colleges* and Edward Fiskes's *The Fiske Guide to Colleges*. This category also includes books that evaluate colleges for their sensitivity toward special groups; for example, *The Multicultural Student's Guide to Colleges: What Every African-American, Asian-American, Hispanic, and Native-American Applicant Needs to Know about America's Top Schools*.

You will need both types of guides. Those containing the college-provided information are good for basic facts—the school's size, the diversity of its athletic programs and student activities, its major fields of study, the number of books in its library, the application deadline. The opinion guides will tell you about the school's strong points and weak points and make judgments about its sensitivity.

In searching for these directories, which are absolutely vital to your college plans, you will run into a problem. In our visits to dozens of high schools—schools like the one you are now attending—we noted that neither the guidance offices nor the school libraries had good directory collections.

What to do? Find a friend who also plans to go to college. There is strength in numbers. The two of you visit the guidance office and the library and request that they purchase at least one college-prepared directory and one opinion directory. Will they do it? You bet they will. In fact, your interest and enthusiasm will please them.

3. **College Fairs.** In most large cities, the National Association of College Admission Counselors (NACAC) and the National Scholarship Service and Fund for Negro Students (NSSFNS) stage a college fair. The groups rent an exhibit hall and then sell booth space to individual colleges. In each booth you will find a representative of the college's admission staff. He or she will have literature and handouts and can answer questions about the college and what it has to offer. These fairs attract colleges. It is not unusual to have as many as 1,000 colleges renting booth space. The fairs are well publicized. Ask the guidance office about the dates. Also find out if attendance at the fair is an excused absence from school and whether the school can provide transportation to the fair. If enough students are interested, have a school bus take you to and from the fair.

4. **College Information Nights.** Many high schools sponsor their own mini college fairs. Admission representatives or local alumni

will hand out literature. Frequently, someone will speak on preparing admission applications or filling out financial aid forms. These events are much smaller than college fairs, but they can still be useful in your college search.

5. **Your Own Mailbox.** College admission offices will flood your mailbox with information if you so request when you take the SAT or ACT (or, if you are a junior, when you take the PSAT). Just check "yes," you want to be included in the College Board's *Student Search Service* or the American College Testing Program's *Educational Opportunity Search*. Also make sure to indicate your ethnic origin, so the college knows what specialized information to send you. Don't assume the college of your choice will send you its glossy brochures, but do read everything that arrives. You never know; a school you had not previously considered might seem just perfect.

6. **Writing to Colleges.** Again, don't wait for information to arrive magically in your mailbox. Write to all the colleges that interest you. Colleges respond quickly to requests for information. If you write, you will get a handbook that describes course offerings, costs, and application procedures. Frequently, a postcard is included for you to use to get more information on a specific major or on financial aid or on housing. Many colleges also prepare special literature that addresses the needs of minority students that they will send you upon request. In your letter, also ask if and when the school will be sending an admission representative to your area. If they do have travelling admission representatives, ask if the representative can visit your home—this way your entire family (including younger siblings) can ask questions and get involved!

In their genuine effort to recruit minority students, some schools make applicants feel more like pawns in a chess game of quotas. Let this work in your favor. For example, if you're seriously interested in a school, ask the college if it will pay your way for a campus visit! Special weekend programs designed to recruit minority students are becoming more popular all the time!

On the following page, you'll find an all-purpose letter, requesting college information.

SHORT CUT STRATEGIES: WHICH STUDENT ARE YOU?

You know now how to get college information. But you haven't yet picked that handful of schools, from the 3,000+ available, on which to concentrate your efforts.

```
Your Name
Street Address
City, State, ZIP

Date

Director of Admission
Name of College
City, State, Zip

Dear Director:

I will be graduating from (name of high school) in June of (year).

I am interested in attending your college to further my academic and
career preparation.

At your earliest convenience, could you please send me an
admissions packet which includes information on academic
programs, minority support programs, special services, costs,
financial aid and housing?

Upon receipt of the information, I will correspond further with you or
one of your admission counselors regarding any specific questions I
may have.

Thank you for your attention to this matter.

Sincerely yours,

(Your Signature)
```

Our suggestions for doing this: Read the following five student profiles. Determine which one corresponds most closely to your situation, then follow the college selection strategy it describes:

Profile A—Career Oriented. You know exactly what you want to be. An accountant. A graphic artist. A systems analyst. A musician.

Profile B—Unsure About Career. You are not sure what you want to be. You are still exploring your abilities and your options.

Profile C—Need Cultural Support. You are very concerned about the transition to college—the move from the familiar to the unfamiliar. You believe the transition will be least painful if you can be with people who best understand you.

Profile D—Need Academic Support. You know you are smart and you have a high regard for your abilities. But you are a realist and worry that your college preparation has been somewhat shaky.

Profile E—The Jock. You are a pretty good athlete. You believe you can use your body to broaden your mind.

COLLEGE SELECTION FOR PROFILE A—CAREER-ORIENTED

Your mind is made up, unshakably so. There is one career for you, and no other, and nothing can derail you from that goal. In that case, you want to go to a college with a solid reputation in the field of your choice.

There are many advantages to finding such a college. The professors will be top experts in their field. They will have good connections with business and industry. And business and industry will have made scholarship money available to the school.

You may already know which colleges have developed national reputations in your chosen field. But if you don't know, here are two things you can do.

1. Go to the Public Library and ask the reference librarian to locate a hefty book called *Gale's Encyclopedia of Associations*. Look up the name and address of the professional association which serves your intended career field. Then send a letter to the association's executive director. The example on the next page is for someone whose aspiration is industrial engineering.

2. In many college guides, such as Arco's *The Right College*, you will find an alphabetical listing of college majors and the schools that offer them.

Either method will give you enough schools to form the basis of your college application list. You can further narrow the list using Profile B techniques (see below).

COLLEGE SELECTION FOR PROFILE B—UNSURE ABOUT CAREER

If you are like most students, you haven't committed yourself to a specific career. You are still looking, testing, and exploring and plan to continue to weigh different possibilities while in college.

You are quite right not to rush into a career choice. The first two years of college are usually devoted to the foundation subjects—English,

Your Name
Street Address
City, State, Zip

Date

Executive Director
American Institute of Industrial Engineering
25 Technology Park/Atlanta
Norcross, GA 30092

Dear Executive Director:

I am a high school senior who plans to enroll in college next year to major in industrial engineering. It is my understanding that many colleges have excellent programs in industrial engineering.

To help me in my college choice, I would appreciate it if you could provide me with a list of accredited schools which offer such a program.

I would also appreciate any advice you may be able to give me on choosing a school, as I am the first in my family to pursue this career.

I thank you in advance for your knowledgeable assistance in my educational planning.

Sincerely yours,

(Your Signature)

languages, math, the physical and social sciences. It is not until the third year that you must declare a major field. That gives you plenty of time.

Your main concern should be in selecting a school with a range of majors. Then, no matter which direction you finally take, you will meet your academic goals.

What's a good range of majors? One that includes accounting, art history, business, communications, computer science, English, foreign languages, history, literature, mathematics, music, philosophy, the physical sciences (biology, chemistry, physics), and the social sciences (anthropology, ethnic and gender studies, political science, psychology, and sociology).

Now you must pick schools that offer these majors.

Here is one way to create a list.

Give yourself a preference test on the topic, "What kind of college would I like to attend?"

Is it a college so close that I can live at home or one at some distance away, where I have to reside on campus. If the college is at some distance, should it be in my state or can it be out-of-state? What do I mean by distance? Under 250 miles? From 250 miles to 500 miles? More than that?

Where should my preferred college be? Would I feel most secure in a rural area? In a suburb? In a big city?

Where would I be most comfortable? In a small college (less than 2,000 students)? In a mid-sized school (2,000 to 5,000 students)? In a large university (over 5,000 students)? As a rule (although we don't like to give in to these gross generalizations), large, urban universities are likely to have more minority students than small, rural colleges. At the same time, many of these large universities focus on research (which often accounts for their first-rate reputations), providing a less than sympathetic environment for all but the most motivated students. Smaller, teaching-oriented colleges can be much friendlier, and more supportive.

Suppose you are a New Yorker, you have asked these questions, and you have answered them as follows: I want to go to a college away from home, but the distance should be under 250 miles. I would prefer to go out-of-state. I think I would be happiest in a big city, attending a large university.

On that basis, and using a map and a standard college directory, you would create the following list of schools:

Connecticut: University of New Haven, Yale University

Maryland: Towson State University, University of Maryland

Massachusetts: Boston College, Boston University, Harvard University, Massachusetts Institute of Technology, Northeastern University, Tufts, University of Massachusetts in Boston

New Jersey: Rutgers University

Pennsylvania: Carnegie-Mellon, Drexel University, Duquesne, LaSalle University, Temple University, University of Pennsylvania, University of Pittsburgh, Villanova University

Rhode Island: Brown University

Washington DC: American University, Catholic University, George Washington University, Georgetown University, Howard University, University of the District of Columbia

That was the first step. In the next step, you begin reducing the list to manageable size. How? By reading up on each of the colleges in a standard directory. If a college, based on this research, does not offer the complete range of majors or has admission requirements you cannot possibly meet, you cross it off.

Then you narrow the list still further. You look up the remaining schools in one of the "opinion" directories. There you may learn the editors are critical of a school's academic performance or consider it insensitive in its treatment of minority students. That research, too, can help you cross off some names.

What's left becomes your application list.

We have prepared some worksheets to help you to narrow your choices. These are found at the end of the book.

COLLEGE SELECTION FOR PROFILE C—NEED CULTURAL SUPPORT

Ever notice how people enter a swimming pool? Some will take a flying dive into the water without first checking its depth or coldness. Others are more cautious. They'll look at the water, think about it, then stick a leg in and, if it doesn't get bitten off, another leg and then the rest of their body. There are the supercautious who sit on the edge of a pool silently cursing every child who splashes water their way before they finally lower themselves in, one inch at a time. And then you have those who never dare to enter—they're the ones who miss all the fun.

Moving from one culture to another is like going from dry to wet. It's easy or hard, depending on your background, your personality, and your level of self-confidence. Some people have the inner strength to deal with the stress that comes when traditional support systems are removed. Most people do not.

The fast learning pace at a college may provide enough shock without having the additional cultural strains of joining a "white society." You may well want to enter that fast learning pace without any additional strain.

How do you find colleges where your group has a sizeable representation? It's easy.

First, establish a general geographic area where you want to go to school, like New York State, Texas, Arizona, or Florida.

Then review the ethnic and racial composition of the student body at each school in the state, using a directory like Arco's *The Right College.*

For example, if you are Hispanic and you want to attend college in Florida, here are the four-year Florida colleges with sizeable (10% or more) Latino student populations:

Barry University	Orlando College
Briarcliffe College	St. Thomas University
Florida International University	Tampa College
Miami Christian College	University of Miami
Nova University	

If your preference was for a school in Texas, you would find nearly fifty four-year colleges with sizeable Hispanic student populations. They include:

Angelo State University	Southwestern University
Central Texas College	Sul Ross State University
Galveston College	Texas A&M, Corpus Christi
Lee College	University of Houston, Downtown
Odessa College	University of Texas, Austin
Our Lady of the Lake University	University of Texas, Brownsville
St. Edwards University	University of Texas, El Paso
St. Mary's University	University of Texas, San Antonio
Southwest Texas State University	Western Texas College

You can also find large Latino groups at Crichton College in Tennessee, the University of Southern Colorado, the University of New Mexico, nearly all of the CUNY (City University of New York) schools and most of the "CalState" schools. This is by no means the end of the list— just a few names to get you started.

Now check the "personalities" of these schools in one of the opinion directories. Also check them for their range of majors and admission requirements. Write to the schools and ask about their minority support systems. Ask especially about mentor programs (pairing you with community leaders, faculty members, or other students), and minority student orientation programs. Also ask about the number of minority faculty and administrators at the school. This will tell you quite a bit about the school's commitment to minorities on campus. Finally, if you're active in your church, find out if there's a similar congregation in the school's community. These checks will help you narrow your list. What's left is a manageable group of schools.

An even easier route to finding an institution that is sensitive to your culture and that focuses on the needs of your community is to look at schools geared entirely to your ethnic group.

Tribal Colleges

There are twenty-six American Indian colleges in the United States; twenty-four are on or near reservations. All but three of these schools are two-year colleges, but they all represent an excellent choice for Native Americans who want to be sure their school is sensitive to their culture and their own sense of traditional values. Tribal Colleges strive to give students a quality education while teaching them to preserve and enhance their heritage and culture. Enrollments range from 80 to 1,800 students; most are in Montana or North or South Dakota; unfortunately, nearly all are poorly financed. More than 80% of those who graduate find employment (although the drop out rates are close to 24%).

Some people feel the emphasis on tribal values and traditions may not adequately prepare students for work. Others argue that the Tribal College's sensitivity to the student's needs gives them the confidence to aim for even higher goals. For more information on Tribal Colleges, contact the American Indian College Fund, 1-800-776-FUND, or write them at AICF, 21 West 68th Street, New York, NY 10023.

Historically Black Colleges and Universities (HBCUs)

Students do best in environments where they feel comfortable—socially and intellectually—which means students who need more reassurance and reaffirmation, or who lack self-confidence or self-esteem, might consider an HBCU. There are over 105 HBCUs (some public, some private) in all, located in 19 different states. HBCUs, however, are not for everyone. Here are some pros and cons to help you weigh your decision.

Advantages. Students attending HBCUs are likely to find more African-American role models and better networking opportunities with African-American graduates. Their education will stress more Afrocentric themes. They'll encounter little or no racism, which can be very important as adjusting to college life may be difficult enough without worrying about racial pressures, or feeling as though you always have to prove yourself. Finally, research shows that black students do better at HBCUs. They are more likely to finish their degrees in four years, and more likely to go on to graduate school than their counterparts at predominantly white schools. There's also a link between minority student success and the number of minority faculty at a school.

Disadvantages. Students at HBCUs will not be interacting with a racially diverse group of students, which could make it more difficult to adjust to "the real world" after graduation. Also, for the most part, predominantly white colleges are better off financially than HBCUs, which translates into better academic resources and facilities. "I don't want to go to a predominantly black college," said one 18-year-old. "We fought this hard to desegregate. Why resegregate ourselves now?"

A few years ago, *The Washington Post* compiled a list showing which colleges received the greatest number of SAT test score reports from black students. Some were HBCUs. Many were not. They were: Howard University, Hampton University, Spelman College, Florida A & M University, North Carolina A &T, Virginia State University, North Carolina State, Florida State University, North Carolina Central, Clark-Atlanta University, Morgan State University, Syracuse University, Morehouse College, Georgetown University, University of North Carolina.

For a list (and description) of HBCUs, ask your counselor to get J. Wilson Bowman's book *America's Black Colleges* (see reference list in Chapter 8), or request a roster from the US Department of Education, Office of Public Information, Washington DC, 20202.

Hispanic Serving Institutions (HSIs)

The Hispanic Association of Colleges and Universities reports on 123 HSIs; schools with at least 25% Hispanic enrollment. Sixty three of these schools are four-year colleges, the rest are two-year. Many Hispanic students are attracted to HSIs because their costs are much lower than at other schools, and their locations permit them to live at home while attending college. For a list of colleges where Hispanic students will be present in substantial numbers, write HACU, 4204 Gardendale Street, Suite 216, San Antonio, TX 78229, or LULAC at 400 First Street, NW, Suite 716, Washington, DC 20001.

Another option for Hispanic students who have reservations about leaving home and their extended families might be to consider one of the country's 200+ Catholic colleges. Since most Hispanic families share the Catholic tradition, attending one of these schools may ease the transition a little.

COLLEGE SELECTION FOR PROFILE D—NEED ACADEMIC SUPPORT

You are smart enough to go to college. But for some reason or other, you got a late start. You didn't take all the academic subjects you should. You had bad instruction. You weren't challenged. Nobody ever mentioned college to you. And so you did not start to think about college until late in the game.

Well, it's never too late. But you will need help or you won't keep up with your better prepared fellow students. The help comes from colleges in the form of learning centers, pre-admission summer programs, reduced course loads, remedial instruction (such as writing and math clinics), special tutors, and the availability of counselors who are familiar with students in your situation and can help you—as they have helped others before you—make the transition.

The College Board's *College Handbook* provides detailed information on the availability of special programs.

Say you are a resident of Houston. You have decided you want to attend a public university within the state of Texas. The chart below shows what you might learn about the special programs offered by the schools in which you are interested:

	Learning Centers	Pre-Admission Summer Program	Reduced Course Load	Remedial Instruction	Tutoring	Special Counselor	Reading/Writing Lab
Angelo State U.	X	X	X	X			
East Texas State U.	X	X		X	X		
Lamar U.	X		X	X	X	X	
Sam Houston State U.	X	X	X	X	X		
Southwest Texas State U.	X	X		X	X	X	
Stephen F Austin State U.	X	X	X	X	X	X	X
Sul Ross State U.			X	X	X	X	
Texas A&I	X		X	X	X	X	
Texas A&M	X		X	X	X		X
Texas Southern U.				X	X		
Texas Tech U.	X	X	X	X	X	X	
Texas Woman's U.	X	X	X	X	X	X	
U. of Houston	X		X	X	X	X	
U. of Texas, Arlington		X	X	X	X	X	
U. of Texas, Austin,	X	X		X	X		
U. of Texas, El Paso			X	X	X	X	
U. of Texas, San Antonio	X			X	X	X	
West Texas A&M				X	X	X	

As you can see, some colleges have an entire range of programs; others do not. In looking at the schools, remember that special programs are a relative concept. Their job is to enhance an academic ability which is below that of the average student admitted. Thus, a student deemed to be in need of special work at a very selective institution might not require such "prepping" at a less selective school or at one that practices open admission.

Therefore, don't narrow your choice of schools by counting the number of special (remedial) programs available. Rather, you will have to decide for each school whether you have the intelligence, drive and persistence to catch up with better prepared students.

Such a judgment may be difficult for you to make on your own. We recommend you sit down with the school counselor and seek his or her advice and recommendations.

You may also want to consider an alternative. That is: Attend a nearby community college for a year, work hard and then transfer to a four-year institution.

Again, a discussion with your counselor is your wisest course.

COLLEGE SELECTION FOR PROFILE E—THE ATHLETE

The Reverend Jesse Jackson said once, "Athletics teach you to persevere beyond sweat and fatigue."

But then he said, "We can't just have skill with our bodies; we must develop our minds," and he told young people to "practice math as assiduously as you practice jump shots."

Be cautious about using your athletic abilities to ride into college. You may end up being used by coaches who take all your time to perfect your individual and team skills and leave you no time to develop your mind.

"So what," you may say. "I will have been scouted and signed to a contract by a major league team. Some players earn over one million dollars per year."

That's true. But for every Michael Jordan, Frank Thomas, Dion Sanders, and Emmitt Thomas, there are ten professional athletes who don't make giant sums of money or last very long in the majors.

And that's assuming they make it to the pros at all. There are nearly one million high school football players and about 500,000 basketball players. Of that number, about 150 make it to the NFL and about 50 make an NBA team.

In fact, only one out of every 12,000 high school lettered athletes will ever make money through their athletic skills; of those, the average duration of their professional status is less than five years. Even Bo Jackson, certainly one of our most talented athletes, has seen his promising career nearly ruined with a hip injury.

A well trained mind is a surer, though less glamorous, bet for success.

Unless you really are a budding Olympian, we would say to you: Go slow in capitalizing on athletic skills. Enjoy the competition and the sweat and the fatigue, but enjoy your mind even more. Use the other four strategies to select a college.

And remember: This country needs thirty times as many accountants as professional athletes, and the typical accountant's career lasts six times longer than that of the professional athlete.

ORGANIZING INFORMATION

After you've used one or more of the above strategies to narrow your choice of colleges, create a folder for each school on your list. Attach a copy of Worksheet 3 (the Application Deadline Checklist) to the outside of each folder. Inside each folder, put:

- Copies of all your correspondence with the school.
- Notes you've taken about the school.
- Material sent to you by the school; its viewbook, minority prospectus, catalogue, application form, financial aid form.
- Photocopies of any papers you've already submitted.
- Names and phone numbers of people from each school with whom you talk (especially admission representatives and alumni).

Do not let anxiety over the number of forms you must fill out keep you from applying. Do not panic over deadlines. By keeping your files neat, and your list of deadlines easy to read and follow, you will remember everything and have all your papers filed on time. If you have any questions about information that goes on a form, ask a teacher or counselor. They will always be glad to help. In fact, some may even give you their evening phone number, so when you're at home, if you start to panic, you can give them a call!

SUMMING IT UP

1. Make sure your guidance office and high school library have current editions of the standard college directories—those that record information provided by the colleges and those that express opinions about the colleges.
2. Decide which college search strategy is most appropriate for you.

3. Use that strategy—and the references—to make a raw list of colleges.
4. Narrow your list by evaluating the school's personality, the school's offerings and the school's admission requirements.
5. Prepare a final list of schools. Make sure the list includes at least one school that is a "safe bet" to accept you.
6. Discuss the list with your counselor.
7. Apply.

What's the time frame for doing all this? September through February of your senior year.

Chapter 6
What You Need to Know About Financial Aid

This is what you need to know about financial aid:

1. Plenty of aid is available to finance your education. But whether you're going to a community college or a four-year university, you must:
   - Apply.
   - Apply correctly.
   - Apply on time.
2. Nothing about applying for financial aid is complex. Don't let anybody tell you differently.
3. Most financial aid, though not all, is awarded on a first-come, first-served basis. If you send your applications off early, in January, you will have a good chance at the first-come financial aid programs. If you wait until late spring, you may not get all the assistance you need.
4. Don't waste time on scholarship hunts. The pay-off isn't worth the effort. You have many more important things to do in your senior year than to look for scholarships.
5. Don't be afraid of loans. Without loans, you will find it hard to fund a college education. Uncle Sam, who stands behind most college loans, has taken the sting out of them. We talked about that in Chapter 4. You may wish to read that section again.
6. Read a good book on financial aid. The best: an annual guide called *Don't Miss Out* published by Octameron Press. Ask the guidance office or the school library to obtain the current edition.

THE PHILOSOPHY OF FINANCIAL AID

Your eligibility for need-based financial aid is expressed as a monetary sum—in dollars and cents. It is the difference between what college will cost and what you are judged capable of paying.

For instance: If a college costs $10,000 and you are judged capable of paying $1,000, you are eligible for $9,000 in aid.

This is important: College costs are a variable. But the amount you are capable of paying is relatively constant. Let's attach numbers to that concept.

You are judged capable of paying $1,000 for college. You are considering College A which costs $7,000, College B which costs $15,000 and College C which costs $20,000.

At College A you will be eligible for $6,000 in aid ($7,000–$1,000). At College B your eligibility is $14,000 ($15,000–$1,000). At College C your eligibility is $19,000 ($20,000–$1,000). No matter which of these schools you choose to attend, your family will be expected to contribute the same $1,000.

The lesson to be learned from this: Your out-of-pocket expense will be about the same whether you attend an expensive or a low-cost school. You don't save any of your own money by shopping for a cheap school.

Incidentally, the amount of your aid eligibility is called your **Financial Need**.

THE COST OF COLLEGE

The cost of college usually includes seven elements:
1. Tuition
2. Fees, such as lab fees.
3. Books and Supplies.
4. Room. Even if you live at home, an allowance is made for room costs. The allowance, however, is larger when you live on campus.
5. Food. Again, an allowance is made whether you eat at home or in the college dining hall.
6. Miscellaneous Expenses. This category includes items like laundry money, an occasional pizza, and medical insurance.
7. Transportation. If college is far away, transportation costs are based on two roundtrips home per year; if you are commuting, the costs include bus fare or an automobile allowance.

Add these seven elements together and you have the cost of college which is used as the basis for determining your eligibility for financial aid. The cost, incidentally, is calculated by the college's financial aid officer.

WHAT YOU CAN PAY

The cost of college is one element of the financial aid formula. The other element is the amount of money your family is judged capable of contributing toward college costs.

How is that sum determined? From information you enter on the **Free Application for Federal Student Aid** (more about that form later). That information covers (1) your parents' income and assets and (2) your income and assets.

For many families, the formula will determine a zero dollar contribution to college costs.

THE FORMS OF AID

The financial aid administrator (FAA), after determining your college cost and subtracting from it your family contribution, calculates your aid eligibility.

Then the FAA prepares an aid package, which—if you applied for financial aid correctly and on time—should, in most cases, cover your financial need.

Generally, the aid administrator builds the package from three types of awards:

Grants and Scholarships. This money is given to you. You do not have to repay it.

Employment Opportunities. This money you must earn—usually at minimum wage. The school will find you the job.

Loans. This money must be repaid. You don't, however, pay interest on the loans while you are a student. And you don't have to start paying them back until six or nine months after completing your college work.

If you are nervous about the first year of college and want to spend all your time studying, you can request that the school initially go easy on offering you work which may take time away from studies.

In that case, send the letter on the next page to the college financial aid administrator.

THE FINANCIAL AID APPLICATION

In some cases you will have to fill out two, three, or four different applications to link up with all major aid programs. The exact number depends on the schools to which you apply, your home state and the programs available in your state.

You cannot submit the applications before January 1 of the year in which you will enroll in college (This is usually January 1 of your senior year of high school). The reason: The computers that analyze your application will want to know exactly how much your family earned in the calendar year preceding your enrollment (1994 for students starting school in September, 1995; 1995 for students starting school in September, 1996).

Here are some tips that are applicable to all financial aid forms:

1. Apply as early as possible. The early bird gets the worm.
2. Take great care with the applications. Follow the instructions exactly.
3. Make sure income information on the application is the same as

```
Your Name
Street Address
City, State Zip

Date

Dear Director of Financial Aid:

I have applied for admission to your college and I have also applied
for financial aid.
During my freshman year, I plan to take full advantage of the
developmental programs your school offers, including tutoring and
special counseling.

These programs, as well as my regular course load, will take up all
my available time. Accordingly, I hope that in my first year, you can
base all my aid on grants and loans.

After I have made the first-year adjustment, I know I will be able to
accept work assignments as part of my aid package.

I request that this letter be made part of my folder and reviewed at the
time you make your awards. Your consideration is appreciated.

Sincerely yours,


(Your Signature)
```

that reported on your family's federal income tax form. The colleges may compare the two.

4. Make copies of all your applications.

5. If a change in family circumstances occurs after you complete the application, you should immediately advise the school's financial aid administrator and the people (the processor) who got the original form of the changes. What are the changes in circumstances? Unpleasant things like death, divorce, disability, job loss.

6. If your parents are divorced or separated, you report the income and assets of the parent with whom you lived the greater part of the twelve months preceding the date of the application. You don't need to worry about the other parent.

7. Make sure you understand the definition of dislocated worker (see glossary). If your parent qualifies, you may ask the financial aid administrator to recalculate your aid eligibility using expected income.

8. If the parent with whom you live remarries, you will have to report the income and assets of your stepparent.

9. If you don't have a social security number, get one now. You will need it for the application.

10. All the application forms you need will be available in your high school guidance office.

11. Don't panic over the form's complexity. Ask if the high school is going to sponsor a free financial aid workshop. Otherwise, your counselors will be glad to help you fill out the applications.

12. Pick up the applications in December and, with your parents, spend some time during the winter vacation getting records ready so you can fill out the forms and send them off right after the first of the year.

13. It costs money to file some of the application forms. Low income students can get a fee waiver. Ask the guidance office if you qualify for a fee waiver.

14. If you want to estimate your family contribution ahead of time (which you should to help you plan), use Worksheet 4. The result won't match the official result exactly, but it will be in the ballpark.

FREE APPLICATION FOR FEDERAL STUDENT AID (FAFSA)

The most important aid application is the Free Application for Federal Student Aid (FAFSA). It links you up with the three largest sources of financial aid—Uncle Sam, your home state, and the colleges you might want to attend. The only thing you have to do is fill out the form, and record the names of the schools and the state which should receive the results. The table on page 58 shows what happens next.

Once the school's financial aid administrator (FAA) receives a copy of your Student Aid Report, he or she goes to work, helping you by building you a financial aid package.

THE FEDERAL PELL GRANT

This is Uncle Sam's largest grant program, and the bottom layer of every financial aid package. You may receive up to $2,340 in grant money, depending on the amount of your Expected Family Contribution. To approximate how much you'll get, subtract your EFC from the

Step One:	You send your completed application to the FAFSA processor.
Step Two:	A giant computer (the processor) evaluates your family's finances and spits out your Expected Family Contribution (EFC)
Step Three:	The processor incorporates your EFC into a multi-part document called a Student Aid Report.
Step Four:	The processor sends you a copy of your Student Aid Report.
Step Five:	The processor sends any schools you designate a copy of your Student Aid Report.
Step Six:	The processor sends your home state's higher education agency a copy of your Student Aid Report.

maximum size grant. For example, if your EFC is $0, you qualify for the entire $2,340. If your EFC is $1,000, you qualify for $1,340.

OUTSIDE SCHOLARSHIPS

If you've received any scholarships from private sources, the financial aid administrator will now incorporate that money into your financial aid package.

STATE GRANTS

Every state has a grant program for low income students. Some states have additional programs specifically for minority students. If you qualify for any money from your state, this will be the third layer of your financial aid package.

CAMPUS-BASED PROGRAMS

These are three federal programs that the colleges' administer; they make up the next layer of most financial aid packages. One program is a grant. One is a loan. And one offers work opportunities. The grant (Supplemental Education Opportunity Grant) can be as much as $4,000 per year with priority given to students who qualify for the Pell Grant. The loan (Perkins Loan) can be up to $3,000 per year and carries a low 5% interest charge. You do not have to repay this loan until nine months after you complete your college studies. The work opportunities (Work Study) are pegged to minimum wage or higher. Students who receive help under these programs normally work from ten to fifteen hours per week.

STAFFORD LOANS AND DIRECT LOANS

If you still need money to help pay the college bills, the financial aid administrator will often suggest you get a Stafford Loan or a Direct Loan. Stafford Loans are made by banks, savings & loans, credit unions. Your guidance counselor will know which institutions in your state make these loans. You then go to the institution, pick up a Stafford Loan application, fill it out, and get the financial aid administrator to certify the size loan for which you are eligible. Direct Loans are made through the colleges themselves. The terms of both these programs are essentially the same. Loans can be as high as $2,625 for freshmen, $3,500 for sophomores, and $5,500 for juniors and seniors. The interest rate is pegged to the 91-day Treasury bill (currently the rate is just over 7%). You don't, however, pay anything while you are a student (Uncle Sam does that for you). And repayment and interest do not start until six months after you complete your studies.

COLLEGIATE AID

Finally, after the FAA has used all the resources he or she can find from other sources, he or she will tap into the college's own pool of money. Some colleges have a lot of money. Others are not so well endowed. Generally, private colleges have greater resources per student for student aid than public schools. The help is usually in the form of scholarships and grants, but can also include low interest loans from the college's own funds, and employment opportunities which are in addition to the federal opportunities described earlier.

In Chapter Four we showed you some sample aid packages made up of all these sources. Of course, different schools have different policies about how aid is awarded. But this should give you the basic idea.

OTHER FINANCIAL AID APPLICATIONS

The most complicated part of the financial aid process is figuring out which forms you need to fill out, and keeping track of all the different deadlines. There are four organizations authorized by Uncle Sam to handle the all important FAFSA—the College Scholarship Service (CSS), the American College Testing Program (ACT), the Pennsylvania Higher Education Assistance Agency (PHEAA) and Uncle Sam's own processor, ED Application Processor. Because all four of these organizations send your data to a single, central processor, your EFC will be the same no matter which service receives your form.

So why are there four services? Partly to spread out the work load. But also, some states and colleges like to have additional knowledge about your family's income and assets to determine whether you're eligible for their own programs. The services, therefore, can package the FAFSA with a supplemental form to get more information from you.

How do you know which form to fill out (and which processor to use)? That's up to the colleges you're applying to, so be sure to find out their preferences. Here are some general guidelines:

Everyone must file the FAFSA to be considered for federal assistance. In addition, some students will have to file the College Scholarship Service's Financial Aid Form (or FAF) to be considered for state or collegiate aid. Finally, some students will have to file the college's own financial aid application and send it directly to the colleges they hope to attend. In other words, you may have to file one, two or three applications, depending on the wishes of the schools to which you apply.

Why so many forms? Simple. College is expensive and there's not enough financial aid for everyone, so schools have to figure out who needs the money the most. Students applying to in-state, public colleges and universities will probably get by with just the FAFSA. Students applying to more expensive schools (e.g., private schools and out-of-state public schools) will usually have to complete the trio of forms described above.

THE FINANCIAL AID AWARD LETTER

If you applied to colleges in December and January and sent off your aid applications in January, you are right on track. In March or April, you will receive a financial aid award letter from your intended college.

The letter will tell you (1) how much college will cost, (2) how much your family must contribute to that cost, and (3) how much aid, and of what kind, you will receive. Make sure to compare all the financial aid award letters you receive. Remember, the cost of college depends on your out-of-pocket expenses, not the school's price tag.

With any luck, your biggest problem may be sifting through all the offers you receive. Colleges are luring academically talented minority students with all sorts of incentives. One student from New Jersey (with a B average) reported over 100 offers—everything from an application fee waiver ($35) to a full scholarship ($20,000). In fact, many of our nation's best schools are using money freely to attract a more diverse student population.

SOME CAUTIONS

All aid awards depend on "satisfactory academic progress." Each college has its own definition of "satisfactory academic progress," but, generally, the term means you must obtain passing grades (C or better) in your courses.

If you don't have great study habits and are not sure how you will be able to handle the faster instructional pace at a college, you may not want to overload yourself with course work in your freshman year.

Students who bite off more than they can chew often lose their aid awards. Don't let it happen to you. Play it safe and go light.

SUMMING IT UP

1. Plenty of financial aid is available! Anyone—no matter what their family income—can afford college; just re-read this chapter to remind yourself how schools determine "need," and rest assured that you'll be eligible for *lots* of financial assistance.
2. Obtain a social security number.
3. If you're required, register for the selective service. Otherwise you won't be eligible for any federal student aid.
4. Find out whether your colleges require any aid applications other than the FAFSA (e.g., the FAF or the school's own form).
5. Pick up the application from your Guidance Office in December and begin assembling data you will need to complete the form.
6. Send the form off as soon after January 1 as you can.
7. Find out from Guidance if you will need a separate application for state aid. If you do, get it and mail it in.
8. Obtain a Stafford Loan Application—if required.
9. Never hesitate to ask your counselor for help.

Chapter 7
A Senior Year Time Table

SEPTEMBER

- Sign up for academic courses for your senior year. Check inventory of college directories in School Library and Guidance Office. At the same time, meet librarian and counselors. Request purchase of references, if needed. *See Chapter 5.*
- Visit nearest Public Library. Check college material. *See Chapter 5.*
- Learn where nearest copying center is located.
- Buy stationery.
- Buy small pocket dictionary. Get in the habit of looking up every word you don't understand and make sure you can use that word in a sentence.
- Obtain from Guidance Office the testing schedule for SAT I, SAT II, and ACT. Write down the registration deadlines and the test dates. While in the office, ask for (1) policy on fee waivers and (2) copies of sample tests. *See Chapter 5.*
- For the next six weeks, take one sample test every week. Make sure you practice using a calculator.

OCTOBER

- Continue to take sample SAT tests.
- Continue to use your dictionary.
- Follow one of the strategies to narrow down your college list. By the end of the month you should have a list of likely colleges.
- Discuss your college list with a counselor. Narrow the list again.
- Write to the colleges you have selected for information and application materials. Use sample letter. *See Chapter 5.*
- Register for tests. Make certain you indicate which schools are to receive score reports (those schools to which you will apply).

NOVEMBER

- Continue to use your dictionary.
- Take SAT or ACT and any other tests required.
- Study material received from colleges.
- Identify teachers and counselors who will write "college recommendations" for you. Discuss your college plans with them. *See Chapter 5.*
- Check Guidance Office and library for financial aid reference *Don't Miss Out*, current edition. If available, check out and read. If not available, request acquisition. *See Chapter 6.*

DECEMBER

- Continue to use your dictionary.
- Send off college applications. *See Chapter 5.*
- Obtain major financial aid applications (FAFSA or FAF) in Guidance Office. *See Chapter 6.*
- Begin assembling data you will need to fill out financial aid application. *See Chapter 6.*
- Find out from Guidance Office if special state student aid form is required. If yes, obtain form and become familiar with its requirements. *See Chapter 6.*

JANUARY

- Continue to use your dictionary.
- Mail off additional college applications. *See Chapter 5.*
- Complete major financial aid form and mail off. *See Chapter 6.*
- Complete state aid application, if required, and mail off. *See Chapter 6.*
- Find out from Guidance Office if your state or city has special student aid program for economically disadvantaged students. If it does, obtain application form, fill out, and mail off.

FEBRUARY

- Continue to study hard.

MARCH/APRIL

- You will receive acceptances/rejections from colleges to which you applied. You will also receive, from these colleges, financial aid award letters. *See Chapters 5 and 6.*
- Discuss your options with counselor.
- Continue to use your dictionary.

MAY

- Make decision on college acceptance and on financial aid award letter. Respond to school with your acceptance. *See Chapters 5 and 6.*
- Advise other schools which accepted you of your plans. Remember, there are students on waiting lists hoping to get into these schools.
- If needed, identify local lenders under the Stafford Loan Program. Obtain loan application, fill out, and send to college for certification. *See Chapter 6.*
- Make summer plans. Employment or summer school.
- Continue to use your dictionary.

JUNE

- HS Graduation.

SEPTEMBER

- Start college. Congratulations. You are on your way!

If by some chance spring arrives and you have not yet been admitted to a school, don't despair. Hundreds of schools report having vacancies as late as May. Some of these schools even have financial aid funds remaining. For a list of schools still looking for students, ask your counselor to get the National Association of College Admission Counselors' (NACAC) annual survey of college openings. NACAC, 1600 Prince Street, Alexandria, VA 22314.

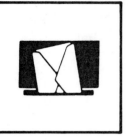

Chapter 8
Application Money, Resources, Writing Letters, Helpful People . . .

APPLYING FOR COLLEGE COSTS MONEY

Before you begin to worry about pre-college costs, talk to your counselor about fee waivers. You should qualify for waivers on testing fees and the financial aid form processing fees. You might also get colleges to waive their application fee, or cover this fee with financial aid.

The estimate below represents the "worst case." In other words, the maximum amount of money you will have to spend on fees and minor expenses in your senior year. This assumes you apply to five schools and obtain no fee waivers.

Item	Month				
	Sept	**Oct**	**Nov**	**Dec**	**Jan**
Buy a dictionary	6.00				
Buy stationery	10.00				
Copying		2.00	2.50	4.00	4.00
Aptitude Test		21.00			
Achievement Tests (3)		28.00			
Mailing Test Scores		20.00			
College Applications				100.00	100.00
Financial Aid Applications					24.00
Postage		2.90	2.90	7.50	7.50
TOTAL	**16.00**	**73.90**	**5.40**	**111.50**	**135.50**
GRAND TOTAL					**342.30**

Here is how you might budget for these expenditures. Start with a $100.00 kitty and add $50.00 per month to your college application fund. Such a plan would produce the following cash flow:

Month	Add	Spend	Month-End Balance
September	$50.00	$ 16.00	$134.00
October	$50.00	$ 73.90	$110.10
November	$50.00	$ 5.40	$154.70
December	$50.00	$111.50	$ 93.20
January	$50.00	$135.50	$ 7.70

What do you do with the extra $7.70? Celebrate!

Remember, this is an illustration of the "worst case." If you are successful in obtaining all of the fee waivers, you need only spend $49.30 or just over $7.50/month!

PRIMARY RESOURCES

The guidance office and/or the library should have the following resources. If they don't, request that they obtain them. We've included addresses for the smaller presses. You will certainly need them to carry out your college selection/admission/financing plans in an informed manner:

Directories That Include College-Supplied Information:
1. *College Handbook*, current edition, published by the College Board.
2. *The Right College*, current edition, published by ARCO Press.
3. *Lovejoy's College Guide*, current edition, published by Simon & Schuster.

Directories That Contain Evaluations of Colleges:
1. *Comparative Guide to American Colleges*, current edition, published by HarperCollins.
2. *The Fiske Guide to Colleges*, current edition, published by Times Books.
3. *Multicultural Student's Guide to Colleges,* current edition, published by Noonday Press, 19 Union Square West, New York, NY 10003 ($25.00).
4. *The Black Student's Guide to College Success*, current edition published by Greenwood Press, 88 Post Road West, Westport, CT 06881.
5. *America's Black Colleges,* published by Sandcastle Publishing, PO Box 370, South Pasadena, CA 91031 ($14.95).

Financial Aid Guides:

1. *Don't Miss Out: The Ambitious Student's Guide to Financial Aid,* current edition, published by Octameron Associates, PO Box 2748, Alexandria, VA 22301 ($9.00).
2. *Loans and Grants From Uncle Sam,* current edition, published by Octameron Associates.
3. *College Financial Aid Annual,* current edition, published by ARCO Press.

WRITING LETTERS

Throughout the text we included sample letters that you can use as you apply to colleges. Type your letters, even if this means getting help from someone at your high school. If you absolutely must write by hand, make sure you use a black pen and print neatly.

- Obtaining Career Information—Chapter 5
- Requesting College Application Information—Chapter 5
- Influencing the Composition of the Aid Package—Chapter 6.

HELPFUL PEOPLE

Teachers	Guidance Counselors
School Librarians	Public Librarians
Ministers and Religious Leaders	Civic Group Leaders

HELPFUL ADDRESSES

Aspira of America
205 Lexington Avenue, New York, NY 10016
Free counseling, scholarship and loan information to Puerto Rican students.

American Indian College Fund
21 West 68th Street, New York, NY 10023
Nonprofit group that began raising money for Indian colleges in 1989.

Hispanic Association of Colleges and Universities
4204 Gardendale Street, Suite 216, San Antonio TX 78229
This association provides studies of the nation's 123 Hispanic-Serving Institutions (HSIs).

League of United Latin American Citizens (LULAC)

National Education Service Centers, Inc.

Suite 305, 777 North Capitol Street, NE, Washington DC 20002

LULAC offers counseling for low-income students and maintains a scholarship fund for Latino students. When writing, include a self-addressed stamped envelope.

National Council of La Raza

c/o Gaudalupe Saavedra, Vice President for Special and International Projects

Suite 200, 1725 Eye St. NW, Washington DC 20006

Sources of financial aid to Hispanic students.

National Scholarship Service and Fund for Negro Students

562 Third St., Brooklyn, NY 11215

Free counseling and referral service for all minority students.

Office of Indian Education Programs and Bureau of Indian Affairs

Scholarship Officer, 18 and C Streets, NW, Washington DC 20242

BIA provides scholarship and loan information to Native Americans.

United Negro College Fund

800-332-UNCF

Nonprofit group that raises money to help African-American students get the education they need to fulfill their dreams.

Chapter 9
Model Programs That Work: A Chapter for Teachers and Counselors

Most of this book is a "why-you-should" and a "how-to" for students, but so many programs have been developed to encourage at-risk students to stay in high school and go on to college, we thought it important to share some of the most successful of these plans with you. Many of them are community- or state-based, so if they've been sufficiently funded, we hope you'll be able to take advantage of them. Of equal importance, we want students to know that many people (both private citizens and public officials) have a lot of confidence in them, their abilities, and the important roles they will play in shaping the future of our country.

In all of our conversations with teachers, counselors and college admission advisors, we've heard a common refrain—education programs should always emphasize a student's possibilities, not a student's limitations. This message is one that Bill Clinton delivered consistently during his years as Governor of Arkansas, and now during his Presidency. His firmest belief is that our nation will advance only when we are all given the opportunity to make the most of our abilities; that the ultimate resource our nation has is the wealth of our people; and that the only way America can compete and win in the 21st century is to have the best-educated, best-trained work force in the world. It is people who lack skills and hope who swell the nation's welfare rolls; and it the most hopeless who turn to drugs and gangs. As Clinton tells young people, the answer is not "just say 'no.'" The answer is to find something you can say 'yes' to.

I HAVE A DREAM FOUNDATION

Multi-millionaire Eugene Lang promised the sixth graders at his alma mater in Spanish Harlem that if they completed high school, he would guarantee them the financial means to attend college. In a class that would normally have had a 60% to 65% dropout rate, 83% of the class graduated from high school (or got their GEDs) and more than half went on to college. His program's success spun into the "I Have A Dream" Foundation—which now has over 10,000 "Dreamers" in 45 cities. Another

100 programs use "I Have a Dream" as inspiration, for example, Project Ready in Newark and Project RAISE (Raising Ambition by Instilling Self Esteem) in Baltimore. In fact, recent estimates show nearly 100,000 students being helped by such programs today. Unfortunately, "I Have A Dream's" success is not easy to replicate, as the program is both expensive and, to be effective, very time consuming. "Sponsors" must put up nearly half a million, of which $100,000 is designated for tutoring and mentoring during the student's junior high and high school career. The sponsor must also work with a project coordinator to assure proper program administration.

THE CHALLENGE PROGRAM, GEORGIA INSTITUTE OF TECHNOLOGY

Five years ago Georgia Tech eliminated its orientation program for minority students, which consisted mostly of remedial instruction, and replaced it with a rigorous five-week summer program of freshman math and chemistry taught by the same professors the students would have in the fall. As a result, the performance gap between minority engineering students and white engineering students has been eliminated. Students feel this "boot camp" approach makes them feel less isolated, gives them the math and science skills they may have been lacking, and makes them more comfortable in their new college environment. Also, the students really appreciate the confidence the school has in their abilities which, in turn, gives them more confidence in themselves. The school's past president explained, "In the past we told them they were dumb, that they needed fixing, and we had them in remedial programs." Now they're being told they're smart, and maybe they just need a head start in learning (and mastering) the system. North Carolina State, North Carolina A & T and Florida State University (in conjunction with Florida A & M) are now implementing similar programs.

COLLEGE/COMMUNITY PARTNERSHIP PROGRAM

Students in twenty low-income communities across the country will receive increased opportunities for college as a result of a unique new program. This program brings private colleges together with community groups to provide both academic and financial support for at-risk students. For example, Roosevelt University will be working with the Chicago Public High Schools while Mount Holyoke College will be working with the Latino Scholarship Fund. The Partnership Program is a joint effort of the Citizen's Scholarship Fund of America and the Consortium for the Advancement of Private Higher Education and is being financed with a grant from the DeWitt Wallace-Reader's Digest Fund.

COALITION OF COMMUNITY FOUNDATIONS FOR YOUTH

Community Foundations make over $100 million in education grants to low income children. This coalition was established with the help of the Rockefeller Foundation to act as a clearing house of information, and sounding board for innovative projects.

THE TAYLOR PLAN

Patrick Taylor, a Louisiana oil man, had a theory: Many kids assume they won't be able to afford college, and see high school as a dead end. There's no incentive, so they don't try. He persuaded the Louisiana state legislature to pay tuition at state universities for any Louisiana student who completes 17 1/2 hours of college prep courses and maintains a C+ average and scores at least an 18 on the ACT, and comes from a family with an income under $25,000. The result—kids are working harder and the schools are getting better. Even parents are getting involved. They now complain about things like "my son/daughter has too little homework." Texas, Florida, New Mexico, Indiana, Arkansas, Maryland, and Oklahoma are considering similar plans.

EARLY IDENTIFICATION PROGRAM

Hundreds of colleges offer programs that encourage minority students in public high schools. George Mason University goes one step further and provides academic preparation and tutoring. Nearly 200 students from Northern Virginia participate. With low grades and a high risk of academic failure, nearly all would be the first in their families to attend college. They enter the program in eighth grade and each summer they attend a three week session on GMU's campus. There, they are coached by university students on their next year's subjects. They also receive regular tutoring sessions during the school year. They get help in negotiating financial aid forms, and support for personal difficulties. Finally, they are promised admission to the university.

YOUTH OPPORTUNITIES UNLIMITED (Y.O.U.)

Through Y.O.U., thousands of economically disadvantaged ninth- and tenth-graders in Arkansas and Texas get the opportunity to experience college life on 14 public university campuses throughout their state. Ninety percent of these students complete high school, and most go on to college. Y.O.U. students live and work on the college campus and earn high school course credit in English and Math. Students also learn about a variety of careers, and receive personal counseling. Colleges provide them with on campus jobs, and as an incentive to the students, many Y.O.U. campuses award college scholarships to participants who return to the camps to attend college. Last year, over $96,000 was awarded to Y.O.U. students in Texas. Because of its success as a dropout prevention program, Y.O.U. is now being discussed in eight other states.

SUCCESS THROUGH ACADEMIC READINESS (STAR)

Financed by the Institute for Community Development, a nonprofit organization in Long Island, NY, STAR proves that high school kids can in fact turn their lives around. There's nothing newfangled about it, just a belief that attention and consistency is missing from many at-risk children's lives. The students in the program are each assigned an academic advisor who follows them through four high school years. The staff also includes a full-time social worker, psychologist, career and college coordinator, program director and outreach worker. In addition to the regular school day, students have an extra two hours devoted to coping with peer pressure, field trips to local museums, SAT preparation, and relentless prodding. Many of the students have family and emotional problems, but the STAR staff deals with these as well. Again, consistency is key. In a way, the STAR program replicates what many students receive at home. The program's success is demonstrated at Roosevelt Junior-Senior High School, a school where the dropout rate exceeds that of New York City public schools. Of the 27 seniors in the program, 25 are college bound. Of the 25 students who turned down places in the program, only two are even still in school.

Chapter 10
A Last Thought

A vendor was selling balloons on the streets of New York. When business slowed down, he would release a balloon.

As the balloon rose toward the sky, a fresh crowd of buyers gathered around him and business would pick up for a few minutes.

The vendor alternated the colors of the balloons he released, first a red one, then a white one and later a yellow one.

After a while, a little girl tugged at his sleeve, looked him in the eye, and asked, "Mister, if you release a black balloon, would it go up?"

The vendor said without hesitation, "Little girl, it's what is inside those balloons that makes them go up."

Worksheet I

What Kind of School Would I Like to Attend?

Criteria	Sample Answer	My Preference
Location?	Large city in the Northeast	
Type of School?	Four Year	
Size of School?	Over 5,000	
Minority Student Population?	At least 15%	
Majors Offered?	All	
Athletic Programs?	Basketball, Track	
Health Services?	All services	
On-Campus Housing?	Coed Dorms	
Special Academic Programs?	Math Tutoring	
Student Activities?	Black Student Union College Newspaper	
Other?	No religious affiliation, Coed	

Worksheet 2
College Information Checklist

After you read this book, and fill out Worksheet 1, you should have a pretty good idea of what kind of college or university you want to attend. Now you must find the school which meets all of your requirements.

The next worksheet will help. Use this form to guide you as you look through college handbooks. First, make a few copies of the form. Then, when you find a school that looks like it might be right for you, read its description carefully, and take notes. Use a separate form for each college. When you're done, you will have a fairly complete profile of each school, and you're ready to move on to Worksheet 3.

Name of School: _____ __

Address: _____

General Information
Type of College (circle):   Four-Year   Two-Year
Religious Affiliation (circle):   Yes   No
Student Body Size   ____Men   ____Women

Enrollment
Asian	____%	African-American	____%
International	____%	Latino	____%
White	____%	Native American	____%

Admission Requirements
1. HS Graduation Required   Yes   No
2. GED Accepted (circle)   Yes   No
3. Required Tests (circle)   ·   SAT   ACT   Achievements
4. Application Fee $_____
   Can it be waived? (circle)   Yes   No
5. Remedial Programs Offered (circle) Yes   No
6. Interview Required (circle)   Yes   No
   If yes, are off-campus interviews
   possible (i.e., in your home town) (circle) Yes   No

College Costs
1. Tuition $_____
2. Room & Board $_____
3. Other Fees $_____
   Total $_____
4. What Kinds of Scholarships/Grants/Loans Are Available? (circle)

       Pell   SEOG   Perkins   Stafford   College Work-Study

       State Scholarships/Grants   University Scholarships/Grants

       Private Scholarships/Grants

5. Which Forms Does the School Require Me to Use to Apply for this Money? (circle)

       FAFSA   FAF   Other _____

6. Special Application For State Money? (circle)   Yes   No

Student Life
1. Student Activities (check those which are offered)

      __Newspaper/Magazine   __Yearbook   __Music/Drama Group

      __Debate Team   __Radio Station   __Cultural/Ethnic Groups

      __Religious Groups   __Student Government   __Other   __Other

2. Housing (check those which are offered)

      __Women's Dorm   __Men's Dorm   __Coed Dorm

      __International House   __College-Owned Apartments __Married Student Housing

      __Special Interest Housing   __Fraternities/Sororities

3. Athletic Programs (list all that interest you)

      Intercollegiate Programs   Intramural Programs

      _____   _____

      _____   _____

Worksheet 3
Application Deadlines Checklist

Now that you've decided on a list of schools, it's time to start keeping track of all the due dates and deadlines. Worksheet 3 will keep you on time! Set up a folder for each school to which you apply and staple a copy of Worksheet 3 to the outside of it.

NAME OF SCHOOL _____

ADMISSIONS DEADLINE
   PRIORITY DATE _____
   CLOSING DATE _____

FINANCIAL AID DEADLINE
   PRIORITY DATE _____
   CLOSING DATE _____

	DATE DUE	DATE SENT
APPLICATION FORM	_____	_____
APPLICATION FEE	_____	_____
ESSAY	_____	_____
HIGH SCHOOL TRANSCRIPT or GED RESULTS	_____	_____
TEST SCORES	_____	_____
ACT	_____	_____
SAT I	_____	_____
SAT II	_____	_____
OTHER	_____	_____

LETTERS OF RECOMMENDATION

Name	Date Requested		
_____	_____	_____	_____
_____	_____	_____	_____
_____	_____	_____	_____

	DATE DUE	DATE SENT
INTERVIEW (if required)	_____	_____
CAMPUS VISIT (if required)	_____	_____
FINANCIAL AID APPLICATION	_____	_____
OTHER	_____	_____

Worksheet 4

Family Contribution for Dependent Student** (1995/96 Academic Year)

PARENTS' CONTRIBUTION FROM INCOME

1. Parents' Adjusted Gross Income .... $_____
2. Parents' Untaxed Social Security Benefits.. $_____
3. Parents' Aid to Families With Dependent Children Benefits. .... $_____
4. Parents' Other Nontaxable Income. This may include child support received, worker's compensation, disability payments, welfare benefits, tax-exempt interest income, housing, food and living allowances for military, clergy or others......................... $_____
5. Untaxed IRA, KEOGH, and 401(k) payments made by parents....... $_____
6. **Total Income.** Add Lines 1 through 5... $_____
7. US and State Income Taxes paid. .... $_____
8. Social Security Taxes paid .... $_____
9. Child Support paid by you for another child.................................... $_____
10. Income Protection Allowance from Table A...................................... $_____
11. Employment Expense Allowance. If both parents work, enter 35% of the lower income or $2,500, whichever is less. If your family has a single head of household who works, enter 35% of that income or $2,500, whichever is less. .... $_____
12. **Total Allowances.** Add Lines 7 through 11..................................... $_____
13. **Parents' Available Income.** Line 6 minus Line 12 .... $_____

PARENTS' CONTRIBUTION FROM ASSETS*

14. Cash and Bank Accounts... $_____
15. Other Real estate, investments, stocks, bonds, trust funds, commodities, precious metals (less any investment debt).............. $_____
16. Business and/or Commercial Farm Net Worth from Table B. .... $_____
17. **Total Assets.** Add Lines 14 through 16.. $_____
18. Asset Protection Allowance. From Table C...................................... $_____
19. Discretionary Net Worth. Line 17 minus Line 18............................ $_____
20. **CONTRIBUTION FROM ASSETS.** Multiply Line 19 by 12%. If negative, enter $0.. $_____

PARENTAL CONTRIBUTION

21. Adjusted Available Income. Add Lines 13 and 20..........................$_____
22. **PARENT CONTRIBUTION.** From Table D. If negative, enter 0. ..$_____
23. Number in College Adjustment. Divide Line 22 by the number in college (at least half-time) at the same time. Quotient is the contribution for each student..$_____

STUDENT'S CONTRIBUTION FROM INCOME

24. Student's Adjusted Gross Income..$_____
25. Untaxed Social Security Benefits ....$_____
26. Other Untaxed income and benefits. See line 4. Also include cash support paid on your behalf from non-custodial parent or any other person...$_____
27. Total Income. Add lines 24, 25, and 26. ....$_____
28. US Income Taxes paid..$_____
29. State Income Taxes paid. ....$_____
30. Social Security Taxes paid. ....$_____
31. Income Protection Allowance. Enter $1,750. ....$_____
32. Total Allowances. Add Lines 28 through 31.................................$_____
33. Students Available Income. Line 27 minus Line 32.......................$_____
34. **STUDENT'S CONTRIBUTION FROM INCOME.** Multiply Line 33 by 50%. ....$_____

STUDENT'S CONTRIBUTION FROM ASSETS*

35. Add all of student's assets—cash, savings, trusts, investments, real estate (less any investment debt)......................................$_____
36. **STUDENT'S CONTRIBUTION FROM ASSETS.** Take 35% of Line 35. ....$_____

FAMILY CONTRIBUTION

37. If one student is in college, add lines 22, 34, and 36.........................$_____
38. If two or more students are in college at the same time, add for each, Lines 23, 34, and 36...$_____

*Contribution from student and parent assets will equal $0 if Parents' AGI (Line 1) is less than $50,000 and the family was eligible to file a 1040A, 1040 EZ, or no tax return at all.

**Independent students (see glossary for definition) will have to consult a book like *Don't Miss Out* to calculate their expected family contribution.

REFERENCE TABLES

Table A—Income Protection Allowance

Family Members (Including Student)	Allowance
2	$11,150
3	13,890
4	17,150
5	20,240
6	23,670
Each Additional	2,670

Note: *For each student over one in college, subtract $1,900 from the appropriate maintenance allowance.*

Table B—Adjustment of Business/Farm Net Worth

Net Worth of Business/Farm	Adjustment
To $80,000	40% of Net Worth
$80,001 to $240,000	$32,000, plus 50% of NW over $80,000
$240,001 to $400,000	$112,000, plus 60% of NW over $240,000
$400,001 or more	$208,000 plus 100% of NW over $400,000

Table C—Asset Protection Allowance

Age of Older Parent	Two-Parent Family	One Parent Family
40-44	$36,100	$25,300
45-49	40,900	28,300
50-54	46,700	31,700
55-59	54,100	36,000
60-64	63,400	41,300
65 plus	70,200	45,100

Table D—Parent Contribution

Adjusted Available Income (AAI)	Parent Contribution
To minus $3,409	-$750 (negative figure)
Minus $3,409 to plus $10,000	22% of AAI
$10,001 to $12,500	$2,200 plus 25% of AAI over $10,000
$12,501 to $15,100	$2,825 plus 29% of AAI over $12,500
$15,101 to $17,600	$3,579 plus 34% of AAI over $15,100
$17,601 to $20,100	$4,429 plus 40% of AAI over $17,600
$20,101 or more	$5,429 plus 47% of AAI over $20,100

Calculations

Glossary

Academic Advisor. Individual (usually a member of the school's faculty or staff) who helps students decide what courses to take and choose a major field of study. Academic advisors also make certain students fulfill graduation requirements and give guidance when the student has academic difficulties.

Academic Year. The period of time during which formal instruction is offered. It usually lasts from September to May or June. The period from June through August is not generally considered part of the academic year, even if summer sessions are held.

Accreditation. Recognition by an official agency that an institution has met certain academic standards.

Achievement Test. See SAT II.

ACT. Standardized test administered by the American College Testing service that measures proficiency in English, Math, Reading and Science Reasoning. The ACT is required for admission to many colleges, especially those in the Midwest and the South. Scores on the test range between 1 and 36, with 20.7 being the national average.

Advisor. One who guides a student through his or her college years. See Academic Advisor.

Alumni. People who have graduated from a college or university.

Applicant Pool. The group of student applicants from which a selection committee must choose an incoming freshman class.

Application Fee. The sum of money charged by many schools to cover the cost of handling student applications. Fees range from $10 to $50, and at some schools may be waived.

Assistantship. Financial aid given to a student in exchange for work. The work is generally offered by an academic department. Students seeking assistantships should contact the department in which they want to work rather than the school's financial aid office.

Associate Degree. A degree awarded upon completion of a two-year program of study by a community college or junior college.

Audit. To take a course for informational purposes only and not to receive a grade. Auditing students are generally not required to take examinations and in many institutions are not required to turn in written assignments.

Baccalaureate Degree. A degree awarded upon completion of a four-year program of study by a college or university.

Bachelor's Degree. See Baccalaureate Degree.

Basic Educational Opportunity Grant (BEOG). See Pell Grant.

Bulletin. See Catalogue.

Bursar. The school treasurer. This is the person at a college to whom a student pays tuition and fees.

Calendar. The formal schedule used to tell students of the major events taking place during the academic year.

Campus. The physical grounds and buildings of an institution. A campus map will show students where various classes and other events are held.

Campus Based Aid. Federal student aid money administered by the college's financial aid office. Programs include Work Study, the Perkins Loan, and Supplemental Educational Opportunity Grants (SEOG).

Candidate Notification Date. The day by which an institution lets applicants know of its admission decisions.

Candidate Reply Date. The day (usually May 1) by which students must let colleges know their enrollment intentions. At that time, most colleges require students to make a deposit of $100 to $300 to reserve their place in the incoming class.

Catalogue. A book describing an institution's courses, regulations, tees, tuition, faculty, location, entrance and other academic requirements, and scholarship and financial aid information.

Class. This word has several definitions. It can refer to a course of instruction (English class); it can refer to a group of students taking a particular course together (class of English students); or it can mean all the students who are in the same year of study (the senior class).

Class Rank. The academic standing of a student in relation to other students taking the same program at the same school in a particular academic year. For example, the student whose grades place him or her exactly halfway between the first and last person in an engineering program of one hundred people would have class rank of 50/100.

College. The word has two meanings. College can refer to a small, four year, post-secondary institution or it can refer to a division within a large university (the College of Arts and Sciences).

College Scholarship Service (CSS). A program of the College Board whose purpose it is to process the Financial Aid Form (FAF) and the FAFSA.

Commencement. The ceremonies held upon completion of a student's studies and the beginning (commencement) of the rest of his or her life. Also called graduation.

Community College. An institution that offers a two-year program of study.

Comprehensive Examination. A thorough examination often given to students at the end of their studies to determine their knowledge of their major. At many institutions, students must pass "comps" to graduate.

Conditional Admission. An act by which a school accepts a student even though that student has not met the minimum admission requirements. In return, the student must first enroll in remedial courses or maintain a minimum grade point average.

Congressional Methodology. See Federal Methodology.

Consortium. Colleges that have joined together to make their collective resources available to all students.

Cooperative Education. A program whereby students alternate periods of study with periods of employment at a job obtained by the school for the student. The job is usually in a field related to the student's major.

Core Curriculum. Literally, the heart of a program of study. Many schools require students to take a sampler of courses (known as distribution requirements) before they graduate to ensure they receive a well-rounded education.

Course Load. The number of courses a student takes during the term. A full-time student generally carries a load of four to six courses per term.

Credit. A numerical value assigned to each course, depending upon its academic demands. An advanced history course that meets four hours a week might be worth four credits while an introductory accounting course that meets two hours a week might be worth just three credits. A student must earn a specified number of credits before he or she will be allowed to graduate. The number of credits given for a particular course is contained in the institution's catalogue or bulletin.

Credit by Examination. Many institutions will allow students to earn credits without taking a course if they are successful in passing an examination that covers the material presented in the course.

Cum Laude. With Honors. Students who maintain a high grade point average can graduate "cum laude." Requirements for this honor vary from school to school.

Curriculum. The course of study offered at an academic institution. There will be one curriculum (series of courses) required for electrical engineers and another required for liberal arts majors.

Dean. The administrative head of a university, its faculty, or any one of its divisions.

Dean's List. A listing of students who receive special recognition for academic excellence. Criteria for the dean's list vary among institutions and programs. An honor roll.

Dependent Student. A dependent student, for purposes of financial aid eligibility, is anyone who does not meet the requirements for independent student status (see independent student).

Direct Student Loans. Money students borrow directly from Uncle Sam at favorable interest rates. The loan is subsidized by Uncle Sam and carries similar terms as the Stafford loan. The main difference? Students apply for the loan via their college rather than a bank. Not all schools participate in this program.

Dislocated Worker. This category is defined by individual state agencies in accordance with Title III of the Job Training Partnership Act. To see if you qualify, check with your state's employment service. In general, however, "dislocated worker" refers to an individual who has been:
(1) fired OR
(2) laid off as part of a permanent factory closing OR
(3) self-employed (including farmers) but is now unemployed because of a natural disaster or poor economic conditions within the community.

Dormitory. A building on campus used to house students.

Dropout. A student who leaves school with no intention of returning.

Early Action. A process by which students learn of a school's admission decision before the official candidate notification date. Unlike candidates for early decision, students who participate in early action are not required to accept the offer or withdraw their other applications.

Early Admission. Students who are offered early admission may begin their college work before they graduate from high school.

Early Decision. A process by which students submit a college application in November or December and learn of their acceptance in December or January. If admitted, the students MUST withdraw their other applications and accept the school's offer. You may only apply for early decision to one school, thus it is recommended only if you have no doubts about where you want to attend college.

Elective. A course students may choose (elect) to take which is not part of the required curriculum.

Endowment. Money or property that belongs to a school and provides that school with income.

Enrollment Deposit. Money a student gives to the college to reserve his or her spot in the incoming class. This deposit (generally $100 to $300) is not refundable should the student decide to enroll elsewhere.

Expected Family Contribution (EFC). The amount of money a family is expected to contribute to college expenses regardless of where the student decides to enroll. Family contribution is determined by a federally approved formula, not the organizations that process financial aid applications.

Faculty. The group of professors and instructors who make up the teaching staff of an institution.

Federal Methodology. The government approved formula for determining a family's contribution to college costs is based on its income and assets. Previously known as the Congressional Methodology, and before that, the Uniform Methodology.

Fellowship. A financial grant given to a student in support of his or her research.

Final Exam. An examination taken by students at the end of each term in each of their classes to test their knowledge of the material covered in class during the term. Grades on finals generally carry more weight than other grades received during the term.

Financial Aid (Assistance). Money awarded to students so they may pay for their college education.

Financial Aid Form (FAF). The form processed by the College Scholarship Service (CSS) to determine a family's expected contribution to college costs. The CSS is a program of the College Board.

Financial Aid Package. The composition of grants, loans, and work opportunities developed by a school's financial aid administrator to help the student pay for college. Two financial aid packages may be worth the same amount of money, but one may contain mostly grants, while the other contains mostly loans. Compare financial aid packages carefully (grants are better than loans).

4-1-4 Calendar. An academic year divided into four-month, one-month, and four-month semesters.

Fraternity. Social organization of male students identified by letters of the Greek alphabet.

Free Application for Federal Student Aid (FAFSA). The federal form a student must fill out if he or she wants to be considered for federal student aid programs. The FAFSA can also qualify a student for state based aid or institutional aid, although sometimes a student must also fill out an FAF, or institutional aid application.

Freshman. An undergraduate student who has started college but has not completed his or her first full academic year. May also be used to classify a student in the first year of high school.

Full Load. A certain minimum number of courses a student must take to be considered a full-time student.

General Education Development (GED) Exam. Tests given to students who have not completed high school to determine whether they are eligible for a high school equivalency diploma.

Grade. The number or letter given to evaluate a student's performance on an assignment, examination, or an entire course.

Grade-Point Average (GPA). An average grade derived from a formula that considers grades received and number of credit hours for each course taken. The GPA is used to determine who should be on the dean's list and who should be on probation or suspended. It is also to calculate a student's class rank.

Graduate. Three meanings. Graduate can refer to the level of study beyond the baccalaureate. Graduate can also refer to a person who has successfully completed high school or college. Finally, graduate may be used as a verb to describe the act of receiving a high school or college diploma.

Graduation. See Commencement.

Grant. Money that does not have to be repaid.

Guaranteed Student Loan. See Stafford Loan.

Humanities. The branch of learning that constitutes the backbone of the liberal arts education. For example, art history, languages, literature, and philosophy.

Independent Student. Any student who will be at least 24 years of age by December 31 of the award year (December 31, 1995 for the 1995-96 academic year) may be considered "independent" for the purposes of financial aid eligibility. A student under the age of 24 may be considered "independent" only if he or she meets *one* of the following criteria:

1. is a veteran of the U.S. Armed Forces.
2. is an orphan or ward of the court.
3. has legal dependents other than a spouse.
4. is married.
5. is a graduate student.
6. is judged independent by the financial aid administrator based on documented unusual circumstances.

Interdisciplinary Study. An academic program that involves taking courses in two or more areas of study. For example, American Studies might include American History, American Literature, and Political Science.

Junior. An undergraduate student in his or her third full year of college. May also be used to classify a student in the third year of high school.

Liberal Arts. A program of study that strives to develop general intellectual ability and cultural concern. This is distinguished from programs that emphasize practical or professional training.

Loan. A sum of money that must be repaid.

Magna cum Laude. With High Honors. Students who maintain a high grade point average can graduate "Magna cum Laude." Requirements for this honor vary from school to school.

Major. The field or subject a student choses as his or her principal area of study. For example, mathematics, engineering, economics, anthropology, biology, art, French.

Matriculation. Enrollment in a college or university.

Mentor. A trusted person who encourages, advises and guides a student during his or her college and professional years.

Midterm. The halfway point of an academic term. Students frequently take midterm examinations to measure their progress in a subject.

Minor. A subject or field a student has chosen as an area of study secondary to his or her major.

National Direct Student Loan (NDSL). See Perkins Loan.

Need Analysis. The process that determines a student's ability to pay for college.

Open Admission. Also, Open Door Admission. A policy upheld by some schools that allows anyone to enroll regardless of their academic qualifications (although some schools do require a high school diploma).

Orientation. A period of time (usually 2-4 days) in which students are introduced to the college, its programs, and its facilities. Orientation usually occurs before the start of classes. If you're nervous about college, look for schools with minority student orientations, or at least schools with well structured orientation programs.

Pass/Fail Grading. Some schools will allow students to take a few courses for credit and no grade (just a "pass" if you complete the course requirements successfully, or a "fail" if you do not).

Pell Grant. Uncle Sam's largest grant program. Pell grants are for undergraduates only.

Perkins Loan. A low-interest (5%) loan program funded by the federal government and administered by the colleges on a first-come, first-served basis.

Placement Office. An office that provides students with career information and helps them find jobs during the summer and when they graduate.

Post-secondary Education. Any education that goes beyond the high school level.

Preliminary Scholastic Aptitude Test/National Merit Scholarship Qualifying Test (PSAT/NMSQT). An exam taken during a student's junior year of high school. It provides good practice for the SAT and qualifies students for the National Merit Scholarship competition, the National Achievement Scholarship Program for Outstanding Negro Students, and the National Hispanic Recognition Program.

Prerequisite. A course which a student must complete before being permitted to enroll in another (usually more advanced) course.

Private College. A school that receives little funding from government sources.

Professor. A person who teaches courses at the college or university level. Professors usually hold advanced degrees in their area of expertise.

Program. The course of study devoted to one major field. For example, a program in art history.

Public (State) School. A college that receives substantial funding from local or state government sources.

Quarter. One of the four terms (grading periods) in an academic year. A quarter usually lasts from eight to ten weeks (see Semester and Trimester).

Recommendation. A letter written in support of a person's college application.

Reference. See Recommendation.

Registrar. The person at a college who is responsible for student enrollment and academic records.

Registration. The process of choosing a program, having it approved, and then enrolling in and paying for the program. Students usually register every term.

Resident Advisor (RA). An older student (usually a junior or senior) who lives in the dormitory whose job it is to help freshmen adjust to the academic and social rigors of college life.

Residence Hall. See Dormitory.

Rolling Admission. At schools that use "rolling admission," a student's application is evaluated as soon as it is reviewed by the admission committee. The student is then notified of the school's decision.

Room and Board. This phrase refers to a student's housing and food requirements.

Scholarship. See grant.

Scholastic Assessment Test - I (SAT I). Standardized test administered by the Educational Testing Service (a service of the College Board) that measures proficiency in Math and English. The SAT is required for admission to many colleges, especially those on the East and West Coasts.

Scholastic Assessment Test - II (SAT II). Standardized test administered by the Educational Testing Service (a service of the College Board) that measures proficiency in a given subject area. It replaces Achievement Tests.

Semester. One of two terms (grading period) in an academic year. A semester usually lasts from thirteen to fifteen weeks (see Quarter and Trimester).

Senior. An undergraduate student in his or her fourth full year of college. May also be used to classify a student in the fourth year of high school.

Social Security Number. A number assigned by the United States government that must be obtained before a student may receive financial aid. If you do not have a social security number, get one from the branch of the Social Security Administration servicing your hometown (its phone number will be in your local phone book). Having a social security number will greatly simplify your life.

Sophomore. An undergraduate student who has completed one full academic year and is in his or her second full academic year. May also be used to classify a student in the second year of high school.

Sorority. Social organization of female students identified by letters of the Greek alphabet.

Stafford Loan. Money students may borrow from banks (and other lenders) at favorable interest rates. The loan is subsidized by Uncle Sam.

Standardized Tests. Tests such as the SAT or ACT that are supposed to measure a student's aptitude and potential for academic success. Their usefulness is a subject of much disagreement.

Stopout. A person who leaves school with the intention of returning after one or more terms.

Student Aid Report. The official result of needs analysis.

Summa cum Laude. With Highest Honors. Students who maintain a high grade point average can graduate "Summa cum Laude." Requirements for this honor vary from school to school.

Supplemental Educational Opportunity Grant (SEOG). A grant program funded by Uncle Sam and administered by the schools on a first-come, first-served basis.

Syllabus. A course outline prepared for students by the professor. Students should use this to plan their academic responsibilities for each term.

Thesis. A research paper that demonstrates a student's knowledge of a specific topic. An original thesis is frequently required to graduate with honors.

Transcript. The official record of a student's courses and grades.

Trimester. One of three terms (grading periods) in an academic year. A trimester usually lasts from ten to twelve weeks (see Semester and Quarter).

Tuition. The cost of the academic program undertaken. Tuition may be paid for each term (semester, quarter, trimester) or for a full academic year.

Tutor. A private teacher who assists students outside normal classroom periods.

Undergraduate. A college student who has not yet completed a bachelor's degree.

Uniform Methodology. See Federal Methodology.

University. A post-secondary institution made up of an undergraduate college as well as graduate or professional divisions (for example, Graduate School of Social Science, Medical School, Business School, Law School)

Viewbook. A colorful brochure developed by public relations experts to lure students to their schools. Although viewbooks do provide useful information, they primarily serve as a pictorial introduction to a college and its surroundings. Students should not rely too heavily on viewbooks for an accurate picture of college life; otherwise they might assume that 90% of all courses are taught outdoors, and that students have nothing much to do but play frisbee.

Waiting List. The list of students who just missed the admission cutoff. Many of these students will receive an offer of admission after the college learns how many accepted accept the admission offer. Some schools rank their waiting list. If you are "wait listed," ask if you can learn your place on the list.

Work-Study. A financial aid program that requires the student to accept employment. The school provides the job which is usually somewhere on campus (in the library or dining hall, for example). A work-study award of $1,000 means the student can work until he or she has earned $1,000.